MYSTERY BRIDE AND MYSTERY BABYLON

Debra Webster

His Glory Publishing

For more writing about the bride and her love relationship with her Bridegroom go to:
Website: https://bridesheart.com

Author page: http://amazon.com/author/debrawebster

ACKNOWLEDGEMENTS

George, without you, none of this is possible.
As I think about my children and grandchildren, I am thankful for
you and pray you will grab hold of the legacy that God is giving
you through this ministry. I see the beginning of it in your lives
and am thankful for you.
Many people have passed through my life. Each one helped God
teach me the truths in this book. Negative experiences in God's
hands are turned into lessons that make me more like Christ.
Positive experiences bring blessings of friendship, fellowship,
training, peace, and summer's growth. Both are needed to
transform us into an image bearer of Christ the Lamb. I am
thankful for all those who passed; through and those who
remain. I need each one of you.

DEDICATION

This book is dedicated to the bride within the church waiting
in the secret place, listening for the sound of His voice.

CONTENTS

FOREWORD

Last days mysteries are being revealed. Only a few are yet to come.

I imagine the Lord is sad as He looks at His church seeking end time knowledge that is sensational rather than that which will ready the church for Him. There is an enormous interest in the Beast, False Prophet and the Antichrist, but few seek what is on the Lord's heart.

First, we understand that the book of Revelation is the "Revelation of Jesus Christ." It is a book revealing the bride of His heart as well. In the opening chapters, we see Jesus, the church, the bride and Mystery Babylon. In the closing chapters of Revelation, we see the bride. Before He introduces the bride again toward the end of Revelation, He judges the harlot. The harlot or Mystery Babylon exists in churches and the world. Think of a double image, a mirror image with a few differences hardly detectable to the uninformed in the church. In the world Mystery Babylon is not subtle. In the church, she adopts the jargon of the bride, but never possesses her faith or devotion.

Revelation shows us that after judging the harlot, an angel who took part in the judgments introduces the bride. This holds great importance. Jesus Christ's revelation of His triumph over everything false also brings forth the bride in fullness. This underlines what scripture tells us. History is His story. Because history is His story, and He chose us, it includes His bride.

When God judges the harlot, she no longer manipulates and controls. The bride company is complete. A tare is a weed sown among the wheat. The wheat and tares must become full grown or ripping out the tare weed destroys the wheat. Mystery Babylon's judgement shows she is a tare. No longer will the tare disguise itself as wheat.

John 1 tells us that our Savior made the world. This passage calls Jesus both the Word of God and the Lamb of God. Throughout the scriptures, God calls His people many things. Among them are sheep, my people, children of God, adopted sons, and so forth. At the end of history, Rev. 21 calls the people of God His bride, the wife of the Lamb and the New Jerusalem. (Rev. 19-21).

Before Jesus, the Word of God created the heavens, earth, and man; God desired fellowship with us like that which the Godhead enjoys. Jesus, by His word, created Adam and Eve and marriage to show us the fellowship that exists between Christ, His Father and the Holy Spirit. He desires this fellowship with us. (John 17) He wrote a book of the Bible to illustrate His intention to us. Song of Songs is more than a biblical book. It is the song above every other song. In fact, it is the song the Bridegroom Lamb has been singing over His bride since before He created us. From Genesis 3 when the voice of God walked in the garden with Adam and Eve until the end of Revelation, the theme of intimate communion is the theme above every other theme. The end of time in Rev. 19-21 centers on the Bridegroom's love toward us being fulfilled because that was His eternal intention in creation.

Rev. 21:9 'One of the seven angels who had the seven bowls full of the seven last plagues came and said to me, Come, I will show you the bride, the wife of the Lamb. 10 And he carried me away in the Spirit to a mountain great and high, and showed me the Holy City, Jerusalem, coming down out of heaven from God.'

Scripture references this holy city in Rev. 21:22. "And I saw no temple in it, for the Lord God, the Almighty, and the Lamb, are its temple. 23. The city does not need the sun or the moon to shine on it, for the glory of God gives it light, and the Lamb is its lamp."

Within this city are the Lord God Almighty and the Lamb as both the temple and the light of the city. The total fulfillment of God's presence, the bride has yearned for is within this bride city. God created us to become this city.

Rev. 10:7 "but in the days of the voice of the seventh angel, when he is about to sound, then the mystery of God is finished, as He preached to His servants the prophets." God is revealing many mysteries over the millennia. We talk much of the mystery of the gospel to the gentiles. The next to the last mystery is the harlot's judgment. The final mystery God reveals is the mystery of the bride. Few teach or preach about the bride during years of church history. But today God is revealing the bride for her time to come forth in the earth is here. The differences between the harlot and the bride will soon become clear to those with eyes to see and ears to hear.

It is easy to lose focus on the priorities of God's heart; the early church did. What lessons can we learn from them and how can we get ready? This book is not an exhaustive study of this question but, examines some of what it takes to get ready.

PART ONE

Chapter 1
The Bridegroom, King, and Judge

Rev. 1:10"I was in the Spirit on the Lord's day, and I heard behind me a loud voice like the sound of a trumpet, 11 saying, Write in a book what you see, and send it to the seven churches: to Ephesus and to Smyrna and to Pergamum and to Thyatira and to Sardis and to Philadelphia and to Laodicea."

Jesus came to the Apostle John and comes to us today with His speaking voice to tell us what we must know concerning the day in which we live. So, He has a message for today's church just as He had a message for the church in John's day.

Rev. 1:13 "Then I turned to see the voice that was speaking with me. And having turned, I saw seven golden lampstands; 13 and in the middle of the lampstands I saw one like a son of man, clothed in a robe reaching to the feet, and girded across His chest with a golden sash.14 His head and His hair were white like white wool, like snow; and His eyes were like a flame of fire. 15 His feet were like burnished bronze, when it has been made to glow in a furnace, and His voice was like the sound of many waters.16 In His right hand He held seven stars, and out of His mouth came a sharp two-edged sword; and His face was like the sun shining in its strength."

Jesus comes to His church in the middle of the lampstands representing each church. The lampstand shows the light of God and is, at the same time, the church itself. A true church carries the light of God. Many institutions today call themselves a church, but they are not a church, by God's definition. Only those with God's lampstand are churches.

The glorified Lord stands in the middle of the seven churches of Revelation. He comes as a glorious King with feet of fired bronze and a two-edged sword in His mouth. The sword is the quickened word of God, the Rhema of God. In Christianity, *rhema* is used to signify Jesus Christ's utterances. He has current messages for His church. He comes to instruct, judge, manifest His glory, and speak to those who are listening. The Lord is in His churches. History is for the end of Satan's reign, the fulness of Christ's reign to begin, and the bride to come forth. Many have outlined the book of Revelation, but I suggest one more outline to consider. This outline lacks parts, but its purpose is to show the overarching purposes of God not to capture the entire book.

- The Bridegroom, King, and Judge. Revelation 1.
- The bride and the harlot within the church (the seven churches through the ages). Rev. 2-3.
- The harlot's judgment Rev 17-18.
- The coming forth of the bride, the wife of the Lamb. Rev. 19-22

Revelation begins and ends with the Bridegroom and bride. God created history for the bride. The Trinity (Father, Son, and Holy Spirit) wanted an intimate relationship with man, like the relationship the Trinity enjoyed (Jn. 17). Man was created by God and given marriage as a way to comprehend the offered relationship. Jesus knew He must die to have us and created us, anyway.

He created everything we see by the sound of His voice and His word's authority. In Revelation by His voice again He speaks words that will bring the end of history, and open eternity to us.

So, scholars call the book the Revelation of Jesus Christ, but the book of Revelation is much more. The book's content is well represented by the outline above. A more apt name is "The Revelation of Jesus Christ and His Bride." We see by looking at the above outline, Revelation fulfills something far beyond the triumph of God. History exists for the bride's sake because of love. The wrap up of history has three major players, the Bridegroom, the bride, and the harlot. Christ destroys the harlot and the Bridegroom and bride spend eternity enjoying fellowship. The beast and false prophet are minor players.

Rev. 1:17 "When I saw Him, I fell at His feet like a dead man. And He placed His right hand on me, saying, Do not be afraid; I am the first and the last, 18 and the living One; and I was dead, and behold, I am alive forevermore, and I have the keys of death and of Hades. 19 Therefore write the things which you have seen, and the things which are, and the things which will take place after these things. 20 As for the mystery of the seven stars which you saw in My right hand, and the seven golden lampstands: the seven stars are the angels of the seven churches, and the seven lampstands are the seven churches."

So, the glorified Christ is holding the seven stars or the angels of the churches and the seven lamp-stands or the seven churches. Then the Voice speaks to His church. True believers and pretenders make up the Church. Christ's words to the seven churches teach us what will and will not characterize Mystery Bride and the Mystery Babylon. Both are present in the church and have been since the first church after Christ's death.

PART TWO

Chapter 2

The Bride and the Harlot Within the Church
The Problem of Getting Ready

Rev. 19:6 "Hallelujah! For the Lord our God, the Almighty, reigns.7. Let us rejoice and be glad and give the glory to Him, for the marriage of the Lamb has come and His bride has made herself ready."

Fine Linen

Most of us are familiar with the biblical statement. *"His bride has made herself ready."* But what does that mean? According to this passage, she is ready for the lamb's wedding, and she is His bride. How has she "made herself ready"? Verse 8 gives us clues. 8. *"It was given to her to clothe herself in fine linen, bright and clean; for the fine linen is the righteous acts of the saints."*

So, He gave her fine linen to wear. This symbolizes the righteous acts she does. She does righteous acts because she is righteous through His blood. There are also obedient actions in response to His voice. We will examine the obedient response to His voice and fine linen in later chapters. Both subjects are critically important to the readiness of His bride. Since many of us live with wreckage in our lives year after year while crying out to the Lord for freedom, how do we make ourselves ready for the Lamb's wedding? For our wedding?

These answers lie in the first part of the book, that is The Revelation of Jesus Christ and His bride. Note the major theme of Revelation is that of Jesus Christ. This unique revelation of Him is unveiling the pinnacle and end of history and His bride, His heart's desire.

First, let us consider the problem that keeps us from being ready and the great price He paid to promise us we could be ready. *1Pet. 1:18 "knowing you were not redeemed with perishable things like silver or gold from your futile way of life inherited from your forefathers, 19 but with precious blood, as of a lamb unblemished and spotless, the blood of Christ."*

Our Futile Life

Since, our family of origin gave us a futile or empty way of life to a greater or lesser degree. Many families pass down much emptiness and others less. Getting rid of emptiness helps us grow closer to the Lord. This is part of our readiness. In fact, this is readiness for intimacy. The Pharisees practiced obedience to the law. They thought their actions were justified. Our calling is to obey out of love. We obey not because we have to, but because we love.

Moreover, He redeemed us from this emptiness with something far greater than silver or gold. Silver and gold are two of the world's most prized possessions. Immature believers still strive after what the world offers. Revelation 2-3 illustrates this for us when the glorified Bridegroom speaks to the seven churches for which He died. Think of the price for a minute. He did not redeem us with the riches of man. He redeemed us by blood! *Cor. 1:23 "but we preach Christ crucified, to Jews a stumbling block and to Gentiles foolishness."* The world cannot appreciate the bridal price. If we receive the world's lies about life and the world's systems of thought, we cannot receive our Bridegroom and understand the price He paid for us. If you read this and believe you do not receive the world's systems, think again. The seven churches did not think they did either until the Lord confronted them with what He saw. He had strong words for many in those churches and encouraging words for others. However, both groups needed to hear His words of admonishment and caution.

Rev. 1:9 "'I, John, your brother and companion in the suffering and kingdom and patient endurance that are ours in Jesus, was on the island of Patmos because of the word of God and the testimony of Jesus.10. On the Lord's Day I was in the Spirit, and I heard behind me a loud voice like a trumpet, 11. which said: Write on a scroll what you see and send it to the seven churches: to Ephesus, Smyrna, Pergamum, Thyatira, Sardis, Philadelphia and Laodicea." 12. 'I turned around to see the voice that was speaking to me. And when I turned, I saw seven golden lampstands, 13. and among the lampstands was someone "like a son of man," dressed in a robe reaching down to his feet and with a golden sash around his chest.14. His head and hair were white like wool, as white as snow, and his eyes were like blazing fire.15. His feet were like bronze glowing in a furnace, and his voice was like the sound of rushing waters.16. In his right hand he held seven stars, and out of his mouth came a sharp double-edged sword. His face was like the sun shining in all its brilliance.17. When I saw him, I fell at his feet as though dead. Then he placed his right hand on me and said: "Do not be afraid. I am the First and the Last. 18. I am the Living One; I was dead, and behold, I am alive forever and ever! And I hold the keys of death and Hades.19. Write, therefore, what you have seen, what is now and what will take place later. 20. The mystery of the seven stars that you saw in my right hand and of the seven golden lampstands is this: The seven stars are the angels of the seven churches, and the seven lampstands are the seven churches."'

In the book of Revelation according to this description, Jesus comes as the Judge and the conquering Lord. This Judge came to speak to the seven churches. Many believe the reference to the angel of the churches refers to the pastor of those churches. Whatever it means, the lampstand of each church is in the hand of our Bridegroom and Judge. He judges the church before He judges the world. We will look at the bride within the Church.

For Reflection

1. What futile ways of life do you practice? Ask the Lord to show you behaviors of which you are not aware of. Write these in a journal and pray for His help until you are free. Freedom takes years, but He is faithful.

Prayer

Lord, help me understand what I cannot now see. Many things influence my behavior. I cannot change what I cannot own. Help me understand and help me change those things that keep me from getting ready for you.

CHAPTER 3

The Bride within the Church

Song 4:12 "A garden locked is my sister, my bride, a rock garden locked, a spring sealed up."

The bridegroom likens the bride to a locked garden, and a sealed fountain. So, this speaks of the bride's purity and virginity. She does not play the harlot with other gods. Thus, her worship is for Him alone.

The bride made Jesus Lord. He is the focus of her life, and she obeys His will. She does not know Him intellectually alone, but heart to heart.

The Parable of the 10 Virgins

On the wedding day in Jewish tradition, the bride's virgin companions (bridesmaids) waited with the bride until the bridegroom came and led them to his house for the wedding feast.

Matt. 25:1 "Then the kingdom of heaven will be comparable to ten virgins, who took their lamps and went out to meet the bridegroom" Revelation compares the kingdom of heaven to a wedding procession. We know that the Bridegroom Lamb is coming for His bride, the true church. The book of John also speaks of this.

John 14:2 "In My Father's house are many dwelling places; if it were not so, I would have told you; for I go to prepare a place for you. 3 If I go and prepare a place for you, I will come again and receive you to Myself, that where I am, there you may be also."

After betrothal, the bridegroom goes back to his father's house and builds on a room or rooms for his new bride. So, then the bridegroom then leads the bride and her companions back to his father's house, where the marriage takes place. Thus, when Jesus said this to His disciples, they understood the imagery. Jesus returned to heaven to prepare a place for us, for His disciples, His bride. Next, He comes again and receives His bride to himself. This is the kingdom of heaven. But so is the rest of Matt. 25:2-13.

2 "Five of them were foolish, and five were prudent. 3 For when the foolish took their lamps, they took no oil with them,"

Not only are wheat and tares growing together in the kingdom, but also the foolish virgins without oil. They have no anointing of the Spirit or the light of God. They have enough to appear as if they belong.

The foolish virgins want the power, the fullness, the anointing of the true bride. But they are not willing for God to break their will to attain this. So, in this passage, He locks them out. In other passages, they bring disorder and every evil work (James 3:14-18, 4:1-10).

Eccl. 2:3 "And I saw that wisdom excels folly as light excels darkness. Folly and darkness go together. Fools commit foolish acts most often under cover of darkness. Wisdom most often works during the day, for the wise do not hide their deeds in darkness. Thus, the wise have their lamps ready."

4 "but the prudent took oil in flasks along with their lamps." The *prudent have extra oil with them. They are not pretending to believe. Time in the secret place has filled and renewed them. So, the prudent have the anointing and the light of His word and presence with them. They received the oil from being with Him.*

5 "Now while the bridegroom was delaying, they all got drowsy and began to sleep. 6 But at midnight there was a shout, 'Behold, the bridegroom! Come out to meet him.' 7 Then all those virgins rose and trimmed their lamps."

Both the wise and foolish slept. But the prudent were ready, and the foolish were not. So, the foolish did works, but neglected the only necessary thing, seeking the Lord. Seeking the Lord, brings oil and light.

8 "The foolish said to the prudent, 'Give us some of your oil, for our lamps are going out.'"

We crush olives to express the oil. Those who submit to crushing the ego, and death of self, have much oil. Those who do not will find the time they spent in spiritual pursuits without knowing Him locks them out of the banquet.

9 "But the prudent answered, 'No, there will not be enough for us and you too; go instead to the dealers and buy some for yourselves.'"

The wise said no in giving their oil to the foolish. They got this oil in the Lord's presence. The anointing and knowledge of His words are not for sale. Preparation of the wise included the price of suffering and devotion. One person cannot ride on another's devotion.

10 "And while they were going away to make the purchase, the bridegroom came, and those who were ready went in with him to the wedding feast; and the door was shut."

The foolish virgins lacked the anointing. The little light they had mimicked the anointing and knowledge of the word. Anointings are not for sale.

11 "Later the other virgins also came, saying, Lord, Lord, open up for us. 12 But he answered, 'Truly I say to you, I do not know you.'"

'The wedding manifests the truth. The Bridegroom knows no pretenders. In fact, the foolish spent little time in His presence. They have head knowledge without heart conversion. Indeed, those who love Him want only Him.

The False Bride

The false bride, the harlot, buys and sells and pretends to be something she is not. She lies even to herself. So, she does not see her fault.

Consider this contrast. An usher seats you in a church. The wedding march begins. A stunning bride stands in the door. She dressed ornately with jewels on her gown, fingers, neck, ears, and head. She lingers at the back of the church for a few moments as the assembled applaud at her presence. Now, the bride walks slowly forward.

"How odd," you think. "She is absorbing the people's reaction. She overdid her jewelry. It makes her look cheap, not pure."

As she continues down the aisle, you see she looks right and left. You cannot hear her inner dialogue, but her body language speaks to you. "She cares more about other's opinions than the Lord's. She is not looking at Him at all."

Listen to her inner dialogue. "This is finally my day. Now I am recognized for the work I did for the Kingdom, for my sacrifice. I deserve this. Look at the faces of the people. They worship me, and I deserve their approval and love."

So, she continues walking, never taking her eyes off the people. It appears she cannot get enough of their awe.

It horrifies you as you notice that under her dress she has on dark underwear. How could she be so blatant?

She reaches the altar and turns toward the people scanning the congregation's faces. Turning, she says, "Thank you so much for making this day possible."

She turns to the Lord as He turns His back and says. "I never knew you."

His Bride

Next, another scene and another bride; she stands at the back of the church. She is beautiful in a simple way. Her gown is white linen, interwoven with gold. His bride wears no jewelry except for the crown the Lord gave her to hold her veil.

Then, as she enters the aisle, her eyes are searching. The bride does not look at anyone but the church front. Scanning the altar, she thinks, "There He is. There is the one my soul loves, the one I must have and cannot live without, my Beloved Bridegroom."

Now, she walks forward, but her eyes never leave His face. As she beholds Him, her face glows increasingly with His glory. He covers her with His glory. The bride doesn't wear jewels or anything to captivate men's hearts. She has already captivated His heart and believes He has chosen her only for Him. He is her jewels and beauty.

Reflecting Him, she comes to the front of the church in increasing glory, and Jesus reaches out His hand. "Come, Beloved Bride and Wife. You are mine forever."

Today, many believe they have time to get serious with God. The bride knows today is the day to press into Him. The harlot thinks she is serious about the Lord, but her motives are not a passion for Jesus, but other passions such as notoriety, adulation of self, her own will, and others.

13 "Be on the alert then, for you do not know the day nor the hour."

No one knows the time of the Bridegroom's return. The wise virgins were ready even though sleeping because they prepared themselves by the many years they sought to know the lord. Then they received from Him the provisions they needed.

Rev. 19:7 "Let us rejoice and be glad and give the glory to Him, for the marriage of the Lamb has come and His bride has made herself ready."

Rev. 21:2 "And I saw the holy city, new Jerusalem, coming down out of heaven from God, made ready as a bride adorned for her husband."

The true bride gets ready. He is her only Love.

CHAPTER 4
The Impostor (Mystery Babylon) Within the Church

She doesn't mean to be an impostor. Mostly, she has no conscious thought she is counterfeit. Call it spiritual amnesia. She believes she is real, but there is no heart conversion. There are so many spiritual forces at work, bombarding the church that all it takes is one crack, one weak block in the city's wall through which the enemy works. Over time, the innuendos and deception work their intended purposes.

The Lord's Bride Replaced By Tares

The chances of what seemed to begin as real being replaced with the impostor bride are great because the world's systems mimic the truth. Slyly, the enemy brings in the half-truths and apathy. The half-truths sound good because we that are a part of the church have yet to allow Christ to conquer the ground in our hearts. It is a process and takes time. Likewise, while we are growing from mental assent to yielding to total Lordship, the enemy sows his seed among the wheat, and the result is catastrophic. The wheat and the tares grow together until the end. The Kingdom of Heaven is like this. (Mt. 13:24-30).

In Bible times, the Romans had a law against sowing tares with the wheat to sabotage an enemy. It occurred often. This occurs in the Kingdom, as well. Many follow the religious system in churches. They even serve in gospel preaching churches. But they do not believe. Jesus is not Lord, and they experience only a superficial change in their lives. They are tares.

Why? Scripture tells us if we believe with our heart, God saves us (Rom. 10:9). The heart comprises our mind, will, and emotions. If our mind believes, but not our will, if we do not embrace Lordship, then we only have mental assent. We have not believed in our heart. Thus, we can honor Him with our lips while our hearts are far from Him. (Matt. 15:8). Therefore, scripture states that even demons believe and tremble. Demons are not converted, but they believe.

The impostor bride and the real bride grow side by side. Tares are only identifiable as we move closer to the time of the harvest. The tare is the grain darnel, which means false grain. In our terms, the false bride applies. Both wheat and darnel look the same until they grow into maturity. Thus, only then can we identify them with certainty. By then, the roots intertwine and rooting up darnel could root up the wheat. So, the two must grow together until the Lord separates them at harvest time. Only He knows who the true wheat, and the true bride is. We may suspect, but God will only reveal it at harvest time.

Darnel is poisonous to humans, causing what resembles drunkenness. Eaten in greater quantities darnel causes convulsions[i] and even death.[ii] Thus, we cannot eat darnel. Scripture tells us God will destroy the darnel, the tares.

Sometimes lessons that teach us what should be are best contrasted with what should not be, like tares among the wheat. The question is, for whose glory do we work? Since pride is the major sign of a tare in the church, this question is important. He calls us to humility and working for the King's glory. Does the Holy Spirit witness this about you or your church fellowship? Listen to what you say to each other, whose glory is being brought forth? Is it God's or men's?

Saving Our Lives Or Losing Them

Luke 9:2 "Then he said to them all: 'If anyone would come after me, he must deny himself and take up his cross daily and follow me. 24 For whoever wants to save his life will lose it, but whoever loses his life for me will save it. 25 What good is it for a man to gain the whole world, and yet lose or forfeit his very self?'"

We see here that wanting to save our lives will cause us to lose them. So, only by carrying our crosses and losing our lives can we gain authentic life requires a death to self that is total. Does your life show this self-death, or are you controlling your life and resisting the plan of God? Do you attend a church that will allow you to save your life or will they help you learn how to lose it? In contrast, we sometimes choose a church fellowship that aligns with our desires for self-protection.

Perhaps you avoid close fellowship, so you do not have to suffer in relationships. You choose to disregard God's call in your life to avoid seeming extreme and facing rejection from others. Likewise, you may ignore certain scriptures because to embrace them requires too much of you. Are you angry with God because of ways He led you which you do not understand?

The self-death needed is a lifetime process. We must be careful not to use that as an excuse to avoid growth. We should heed the call to come and die to self. The exciting part is we become alive unto Him. In contrast, the reward of living for self is death masquerading as life. It's a counterfeit for His life.

The churches of Revelation are examples of what should and should not be, churches commended, and churches warned Throughout history there is a counterfeit of His real, an impostor. There are those who want it easy and think God exists to serve us, make us happy, comfortable and meet our needs. Whole segments of today's church teach this. This belief is big in America, and we have exported it overseas.

The Harlot

The harlot uses the spices in the bride's garden. Those spices speak of His death. That woman is Mystery Babylon, the harlot. In Revelation 13:18 the harlot trades in *"cargoes of cinnamon and spice, of incense, myrrh and frankincense, of wine and olive oil"* She merchandises the anointing, using it for profit. How sad since anointing for ministry help God's people. Anointings can be counterfeit. The purpose of Godly ministry is not to gain fame or fortune, yet this person merchandises the things of God.

The harlot trades in "cargoes and bodies and souls of men." Revelation 18:11-12. Bodies are numbers. Numbers make the work look successful. The more bodies present, the greater the king or leader appears. People are not God's precious sheep to tend with care. They are cogs in the gears of the king's power. They are merchandise, a commodity to use and throw away when no longer useful or will no longer submit to autocratic rule.

The harlot uses the word of the Lord to get her ways; she comes saying, "I have heard from God," and she buys the hearts of people hungry for spiritual reality. Scripture calls people with this problem false prophets. Sadly, they may have carried an accurate word from God, but now they have prostituted it for the praise of men or the riches of this earth. Is there hope for this person? There is always hope. I write this, so we can know symptoms and avoid the causes of this problem in **our own lives** and so we pray for others.

The adulterous wife uses these spices. In Proverbs 7:17 the adulterous wife says, *"I have perfumed my bed with myrrh, aloes, and cinnamon."* Verse 21 tells us, *"With persuasive words, she led him astray, she seduced him with her smooth talk."* She told him she was dead to self. After all, the spices prove she has suffered. She said she heard from God and God anointed her. She told him what he wanted to hear, and he fell for it because he wanted to indulge the flesh. The harlot seduces us into a counterfeit of the relationship between the Bridegroom and the bride. The adulterous wife leads the unwary to her "anointed" bed using scripture to deceive.

Who is this adulterous wife then? It is the person who is worshipping other gods the way Israel worshipped other gods along with the Lord. The adulterous wife worships having her way. Her gods are power, notoriety, control, envy, and a host of others large and small. She knows how to use the things of God to look holy. This is a person who knows the word and uses it to fool many.

Calvary's Incense is on the Harlot's Bed

Psa. 45:8 "All thy garments smell of myrrh, aloes, and cassia."

These words speak of Christ. The adulterous wife has myrrh, aloes, and cinnamon on her bed. The bed shows us this refers to seduction. Cinnamon and cassia are very similar in smell. Myrrh and aloes embalmed Jesus, and were part of in the anointing oil. The adulterous wife uses spiritual gifts and attributes of God to seduce. Thus, we must pray and live in the word so that we can tell the difference between the real and the false. A sign of the real is that you move into a deeper relationship with Him. You die to your own will and become alive to His will.

The harlot of Revelation is a spiritual and political system characterized by idolatry. This idolatry takes many forms beyond statues of other gods. It is the worship of man's choices without God. Because of this, the harlot encompasses the false religions of history, including false forms of Christianity. (Rev. 17-18) So, some who were a part of the Ephesian, Pergamos, Thyatira, Sardis, and Laodicean churches were false believers and took part in the harlot system.

We could view the attributes of these negative images and warnings from God's word and learn what we should not do. These warnings are there to help us, so we do not take part in idolatry. Read them and learn from them. They have value for searching the heart.

But, one understanding is most needful. The true bride has eyes only for her Holy Husband. She is not seeking approval, worldly riches, or the world's offerings. Her eyes focus on Him and, as a result, her heart is His alone. She does not trade in bodies and souls of men. (Rev. 18:11-13) Rather, she loves the Lord with all her heart, soul, mind, and strength and her neighbor as herself. Reaching out to others is to satisfy His heart and display His glory in the earth. Measure your own heart and the fruit of various ministries by this measure. Where do you focus your heart?

The day in which we live will reveal the difference between the impostor and the true bride. In many countries where persecution is a normal part of the Christian experience, only the true bride will name His name. Pretenders are not willing to pay the price of prison, torture, or death to say they belong to Him. But, in countries without persecution, things are not so clear. The suffering coming to any nation is a blessing to purify the church. Suffering brings forth the bride of his heart. It helps her get ready. It brings her into the intimacy for which she was born.

For Reflection

1. Are you following a system or are you following Him?
2. Where do you focus your heart? If you have anything in your focus but Him, repent of this and ask His help.
3. Ask God to help you become the bride church of the last days.

Prayer

Lord, Help!! I cannot do this on my own. My heart wanders, but I want to focus on You alone. I know the single focus of the heart takes time. I set my heart in Your direction and trust You to take me there and to bring me back to You whenever I wander. Lord, I want you be the sole focus of my life.

CHAPTER 5

Ephesus, the Fallen Church

He Sees Everything

Rev. 2:1 "To the angel of the church in Ephesus write: The One who holds the seven stars in His right hand, the One who walks among the seven golden lampstands, says this:"

Christ holds the seven stars (leaders) in His hand. He is near His church. Often, we think of Him in different terms than this. Many leaders rationalize and tell themselves God does not see what they are doing, or He is not that concerned.

In contrast, this passage tells us Jesus knows everything that takes place in ministry. We cannot delude ourselves into thinking we are the exception. People may acclaim a leader, but God knows the heart, for He holds the heart of each leader in His hand.

This comforts the leader that made Jesus Lord. God assures us He holds us when His will is difficult and discouragement reigns.

The one who walks among the lampstands is near true believers. Indeed, we can know Him. He walks among our assemblies. He knows what is taking place. We hide nothing from Him. He can bring blessing or correction.

Rev. 2:2 'I know your deeds and your toil and perseverance, and that you cannot tolerate evil men, and you put to the test those who call themselves apostles, and they are not, and you found them to be false;'

Now the One who is near tells them what he sees as he walks among them. In fact, he knows their deeds. Then he lists their deeds. They toil and persevere; they do not tolerate evil men and do not accept false apostles.

3 'and you have perseverance and have endured for My name's sake, and have not grown weary.'

Again, the Lord tells them they have persevered. They have endured for the sake of the Lord's name, so they would not disgrace Him. Ephesus has not grown weary of serving. Serving is important, but the heart the service comes from is more important than the serving.

First Love

4 'But I have this against you, that you have left your first love.'

Ephesus did much well, but they no longer put Jesus first. Like this Ephesians' church, many today no longer put Him first. They minister much and do many works with great patience, but they no longer are desperate to know Christ. Rather, their passion has waned, and no amount of good works makes up for lost passion. The Lord will have a bride, not a distant cousin.

First-love does not mean exciting or euphoric, although it may contain this. Protos in the Greek is the word for first, and it means foremost, in order of importance, chief-(est) and is the superlative of pro or before. So, first love means the love above all other loves. This is like King of Kings or Lord of Lords. These names are the superlative of all kings and lords. It means our love for God is to be a love above other loves, like the love our Bridegroom has for us.[iii]

5 'Therefore remember from where you have fallen, and repent and do the deeds you did at first;"

Remember is an admonition to return to first works. This is difficult if time has passed since they fell. This is a sharp admonition to help this church listen. God has a plan for their restoration if they/we will turn to Him.

So, what were our first deeds? We must remember and repent. Scripture instructs us and helps us remember. Consider this passage.

God's Wedding Song

Song 1:1 "The Song of Songs, which is Solomon's." A more apt title for this book of the Bible is the Bridegroom's Song of Songs. This is the wedding song our groom sang over us on Calvary. The Bridegroom has been singing this song since before He created us. Something within us understood this love when we came to know Him. We must return to the one who planned and created us to be His bride. In fact, the title Song of Song's tells us this song is the highest song in the universe. This alone is reason enough to return and repent. And His admonition to us about first love tells us we need to love Him with love above other loves.

Song 1:2 "May he kiss me with the kisses of his mouth! For your love is better than wine". Just like Shulamite, when we first met Him, we longed for intimate time with Him. It is so easy to let ministry or good works replace intimacy. People and problems around us are more concrete and immediate. We forget the best ministry takes place through those who spend time in the Secret Place with Him. He made us for himself first and to touch others second.

Wine in scripture symbolizes blessing. We once wanted His love more than any blessing. Do you now seek Him for answers and material things rather than seeking Him because you are desperate to know Him? Have you forgotten that in dry times and times of great blessing, He still must be our first love? The spiritual disciplines of prayer, scripture, solitude, journaling, and others help us through difficulty and blessing so that we could keep Him first.

Ministry cannot become the focus, no matter how much need is in front of us. Instead, we must stay connected to Him intimately. He must be the source of our ministry, or we are in trouble. Song of Songs illustrates this for us:

Song 1:3 "Your oils have a pleasing fragrance; Your name is like purified oil "

"Your name is like purified oil" means to empty out.[iv] His fragrance is pleasing, and He emptied His anointing for us on Calvary.

Song 1:3b "Therefore, the maidens love you."

We must remember Calvary and the love He showed. We love because of His love. If we forget Calvary, we easily forget His love. It can become a fact rather than a love from which ministry and life flow.

Song 1:4 "Draw me after you and let us run together! The king has brought me into his chambers." Do you remember when you cried out, "draw me"? When you found you were in His presence, you rejoiced and could talk of nothing else but "your" Beloved. Where did this passion go? When did this loss happen? Trace it back and repent. Begin again to make Him first.

His Garden

He calls us to lock our garden unto Him. *Song 4:12 "You are a garden locked up, my sister, my bride. You are a spring enclosed, a sealed fountain. Your plants are an orchard of pomegranates with choice fruits, with henna and nard, nard and saffron, calamus and cinnamon, with every kind of incense tree, with myrrh and aloes and all the finest spices."*

Picture the bride as a walled garden filled with marvelous fruitfulness. She is full of spices that are His attributes. How do we humans handle such abundance? Once we have what we need from a garden, we want to give away or sell the abundance to help others. This can be selfless giving or performing for others. If we think in terms of relationships, it gets interesting. Many believers appear to have the attributes of Christ and display how wonderful they are. In fact, they let those around them see their "Christ-likeness" by using what is in their garden. The words they use pass muster but, underneath is selfish ambition and pride. They are using the spices of God (Christ's death) to get the approval of others.

There is another choice. We can keep our garden locked, our spring enclosed, and our fountain sealed. What good is a locked garden? Who will enjoy the fruit? Who drinks from a sealed fountain? How do we give spiritual food and drink to others? The answers to these questions lay in the next several verses.

First, note his description of her as a garden locked. This former man-worshipper, playing the harlot with idols of the mind, is a virgin. She locks her garden unto him. Everything is for him. Others receive help from her life in other ways, but the fruitfulness within her garden is His.

Note the spices in her garden. These spices are in the anointing oil and the incense used in the temple. These are the types and shadows of His death. Workers harvest these with significant cost. They used myrrh for embalming. It was a product carried on the caravan that carried Joseph into slavery *(Genesis 38:25-27)*. Myrrh was one gift given to Joseph on the second trip his brothers made. It is interesting that myrrh played a prominent role in the life of a slave to become a leader. In fact, it plays a prominent role in the lives of slaves who become leaders today, too. Death births a true anointing. Esther used myrrh for six months to prepare her to go into the king *(Esther 2:12)*. The Wise-men gave Jesus myrrh at his birth *(Matt. 2:12)*. On the cross, the soldiers gave it to Jesus to drink *(Mk. 14:23)*. The disciples used myrrh to embalm him *(Jn. 19:39)*. A bride prepared for the bridegroom allows the myrrh to do its work.

Frankincense is an incense tree. The farmer wounds the tree. [v] Only as wounding takes place can she receive this attribute. This spice fixes the odor of the incense and anointing oil. This is a lasting anointing. It does deep work. Unfortunately, counterfeit anointings are fun while they happen, but when the "anointed one" leaves, no real growth has taken place. They smell good for a short time because the one ministering avoided suffering. But true anointings work in lives until we live in the King's presence eternally.

Another spice, calamus, is a fragrant reed and means erect. [vi] In Revelation 11 calamus is the rod that measures the court of the temple for judgment. In the book of Ezekiel calamus measures the new temple. This reed measures us against the measure of God. We often measure ourselves against each other and believe we are better than our neighbor. However, measured against the Lord, we fall short.

Henna or campfire is a shrub with white flowers. The leaves and flowers, when dried and crushed, become a dye for hair and beard. [vii] Even our fruitfulness is crushed that we learn to love Him.

Nard is the spikenard we read about earlier.[viii] This is an expensive fragrance and used to anoint the Lord's feet before his death and burial. This ointment is rose-red and costly.

Saffron is the autumn crocus valued for aroma and flavor and a vivid yellow dye.[ix]

Aloes was a tree the size of the olive and has an aromatic resin. Wounding the tree gave forth the fragrance.[x]

To harvest cinnamon, the farmer strips the inner bark of the tree and dries it. They cut the branches when they are an inch thick. Often, the believer feels as if someone pruned their branches. Pruning is painful. However, pain brings the attributes of God. These spices are types of His suffering and His holiness. If you feel as if God stripped your bark, you are blessed.

So, the question is, if she locks her garden unto Him, how can others receive from her life? *Genesis 49:22 "Joseph is a fruitful vine, a fruitful vine near a spring, whose branches hang over a wall."* If my apple tree hangs over in my neighbor's yard, they are entitled to the apples on that part of the tree. Her garden's abundance is only enjoyed by others, as it spills out over the wall. Everything else belongs to the Bridegroom. This is the abundant fruitfulness of an intimate relationship.

Song 4:15 "You are a garden fountain, a well of flowing water streaming down from Lebanon."

The bride is a locked fountain and a well of streaming water. Notice that the fruitful vine of Joseph grows near a spring. Whatever flows out under the garden gate is the overflow. Whatever hangs over the wall is extra for others. The bride only opens for her Beloved. Because of this, she does not prostitute God's gifts. She never uses His gifts and incense to draw others to herself. The bride will not boast of her Christlikeness. She does not avoid suffering, for to avoid suffering is to avoid true Christlikeness. She wants to know Him and become like Him. Since suffering is a part of that, so be it.

The bride is a well of flowing water, a spring. *John 4:14b "Indeed the water I give him will become in him a spring of water welling up to eternal life."* The Lord is the source of this living water.

These are the first works; first love for Christ, then ministry to others.

Is Your Light Darkness

Rev. 2:5b "or else I am coming to you and will remove your lampstand out of its place — unless you repent."

The lampstand is the light and anointing of the word and Spirit of God. Without the lampstand we have :

Luke 11:34 "The eye is the lamp of your body; when your eye is clear, your whole body also is full of light; but when it is bad, your body also is full of darkness35. Then watch out that the light in you is not darkness."

Yes, deception causes us to call the darkness light. Our only hope is the light of His word by His Spirit.

Lamps illuminate the darkness to dispel it. Indeed, if He removes the lampstand, we will not notice because we have already been embracing the darkness.

6 'Yet this you do have, that you hate the deeds of the Nicolaitans, which I also hate.'

It is good to hate what God hates. God notices this, but our spiritual state can keep this from being to our credit. We must listen to His voice and obey. He calls us to seek Him. Then we will stay connected with our first love. (More later about the Nicolaitans.)

7'He who has an ear, let him hear what the Spirit says to the churches.'

As you read this, the Lord is saying, "can you hear me." Ask God to give you ears to hear.

'To him who overcomes, I will grant to eat of the tree of life which is in the Paradise of God.''

So, we must overcome apathy, good works mentality and forgetting our lover. We must passionately seek Him to know Him. If we do this, we receive the tree of life.

For Reflection

1. Where is your passion for God? Are you as fervent as you were

at first?

2. How can you better enter God's light by spending time with Him?

3. Do you need a balance between good works, your job and time with God? If so, what are will you change?

Prayer

Help me draw near You, Lord. I need You to continue to call me to yourself. I cannot do this on my own. Show me how to have balance in my life, including the time with You. Make me desperate to know You.

CHAPTER 6
Smyrna, the Suffering Church

Rev. 2:8 "And to the angel of the church in Smyrna write:
The First and the Last, who was dead, and has come to life, says
this: Rev. 2:9 'I know your tribulation and your poverty (but you are
rich), and the blasphemy by those who say they are Jews and are not,
but are a synagogue of Satan."

The Lord comes to Smyrna as the one who died and rose
from the dead. This was important because of what followed. You
will note as you read this passage that the Lord has no word
of correction for Smyrna. Instead, He is encouraging them. The
government barred them from holding a well-paying job because
they were Christians. In Smyrna, the synagogue was responsible
for persecution. The authorities murdered the bishop Polycarp
there because of the Jews of the area.[xi]

10 'Do not fear what you are about to suffer. Behold, the devil is
about to cast some of you into prison, so that you will be tested, and
you will have tribulation for ten days.'

God lets them know they will suffer persecution for a brief
period. He tells them not to fear. This church was not worldly like
other churches because God purified them by suffering. He had
only encouragement for them. Though they were poor, they were
rich in Him. They were rich enough in loving Him that He found
them faithful. In fact, suffering drove Smyrna to Christ. First, they
went for answers. Over time, they learned when they looked for
answers, they found Him, and He is always enough.

First Love and Faithfulness
Smyrna did not lose the passion and wonder of first love. Suffering

drives us to God. We are desperate for Him and as we search; we find passion renewed by our desperation. To avoid suffering is to avoid passion. Ephesus struggled with first love because they did not suffer persecution. In reality, suffering is a gift to purify our faith.

'Be faithful until death, and I will give you the crown of life.11 'He who has an ear, let him hear what the Spirit says to the churches. He who overcomes will not be hurt by the second death.'

Some from Smyrna die to remain faithful to God. He was encouraging them to stay faithful. Therefore, He presented Himself as the one who died yet is alive. Smyrna knew a secret the modern church would be wise to discover.

Suffering Is A Gift

*Phil. 1:29"For it has **been granted** to you on behalf of Christ not only to believe on him, but also to suffer for him,'"*

The word granted as used in Phil 1:29 means gift or charis (in Greek). This is the same word for the gifts of His grace mentioned in Corinthians 12. Suffering is a gift, just as His death was a gift to us. By His death, He interceded for us. This was spiritual warfare of the highest level. Sometimes our suffering is warfare on behalf of His kingdom. We love to talk about the gifts of healing or prophetic preaching, but we do not recognize what a gift suffering is to us. Suffering is how we become like Him. It is the way we give up the behaviors that keep us from knowing Him intimately. Suffering tears down the wall that separates us from Him.

As we suffer and die to self, we not only take part in His suffering and death, but we enter the tomb for a season. This excerpt from *Bridegroom's Song* illustrates what Smyrna was learning.

Song 2:7 "Daughters of Jerusalem, I charge you, by the gazelles and does of the field: Do not arouse or awaken love until it so desires. Song 2:8 Listen! My beloved! Behold, he is coming, Climbing on the mountains, Leaping on the hills! 9 "My beloved is like a gazelle or a young stag. Behold, he is standing behind our wall,"

This is the correct picture of the bride's heart. Love for Him cannot arouse or awaken until it desires Him. The bride never loses the desire for Him, but the price of desiring Him in the past was all, everything. It is time for the heart to lie numb and broken for a season. She will yearn for Him again. The tomb must do its work. He is behind their wall. She cannot see Him because the past suffering has obscured Him in this tomb season.

The longer time she spends in the tomb, the more glorious the resurrection and the greater the love she will have for Him as the tomb imprints the lessons of dying, in the deepest recesses of the heart. Time for reflection is plentiful. Deep learning takes place here, although the bride will feel she is learning nothing. In reality, she is learning how to stay dead, how to survive the loss of everything. She is learning to let her will become His will.

What then did she lose? It must have been something precious to produce this profound effect. No, it was not valuable, at least, not to God. He is the one that made sure she lost it. To her, though, it was life. Her identity, however false it might be, died. What takes its place?

Ideals

Her problem has been one of trust. In whom or what has she trusted? If you ask her, she will say she trusted the Lord. That is the correct theological answer, but not true. Each believer trusts in their ideals, expectations, and opinions much more than they trust in God. They trust in them until they die. Dead people don't have ideals, expectations, and opinions.

The dictionary tells us that an ideal "exists as a mental image or in fancy or imagination only:" [xii] In other words, we might call it an idol of the mind. Notice it exists in the imagination only. That means we bring with us ideas of how life ought to be that exist only in our minds. This is where false identity lives as an idea that exists only in our minds. These ideas have no basis in reality. This is true for our personal lives and our corporate life as a church. We often guide our lives more by ideals than we do by the truth. And we expect others to live up to our ideals for the Christian life. We then measure everything based on the ideals we cherish and protect. The church, when doing this, adds things that are tests of the genuineness of faith. We base tests on external actions. This presents a performance-based criterion that ensnares the saints and keeps them from an authentic relationship with the Lord.

Religious life is prone to this. We read one scripture and form a new ideal because we interpret scripture based on our ideals. Ideals cause us to put expectations upon others and upon God. We expect both man and God to act as we have idealized. Since our basic premises are wrong, idealism must die for us to see God as He is and see our brothers as they are.

Another word to consider in this context is the word real. Real refers to things permanent. It is not an illusion. It is not fraudulent. In place of clinging to ideals, we are to become real. We are to lay aside our illusory idols.

The Shadows We Cling To
In the New Testament, the word truth means, "not concealed.[xiii] In other words, real. Contrast this with shadow.

Heb. 10:1 "For the Law, since it has only a shadow of the good things to come and not the very form of things, can never, by the same sacrifices which they offer continually year by year, make perfect those who draw near." NAS.

Not only is the law a shadow, but the temple and tabernacle layout are shadows of our increasing intimacy with the Lord as we grow. Shadows show us the shape of things, but are not the things themselves.

Shadows offer benefits. There is shade or protection provided, but the shadow is not the object providing the shade or protection. There are shadows in the scripture, but the reality of them is found in Jesus Christ.

Our ideals are shadows. The Israelites worshipped their shadows, their ideas of what He was like. So, do we. When He shows up in our lives, we do not recognize Him because our ideals about Him have blinded us. If He causes the loss of these ideals, we are not losing something real, but they are important to us. We have trusted in these instead of God, and we experience catastrophic suffering to lose them. They are our lives, our identity, that by which we guide life.

We are like the man in Jeremiah 17:5 *"Cursed is the man who trusts in man, who depends on flesh for his strength, and whose heart turns away from the Lord.* We, the bride, have trusted in our self, and our ideals rather than the Lord. Wrongfully, we have depended upon our flesh for strength, or upon the flesh of others who seem to live up to our ideal.

Jeremiah 17: 1-2 says," Judah's sin is engraved with an iron tool, inscribed with a flint point, on the tablets of their hearts and on the horns of their altars. Even their children remember their altars and their Ashram poles."

These ideals inscribe themselves upon our hearts. We worship our ideas. They are upon the horns of our altars. They are our idols, and our sin affects our children. Unfortunately, our ideals have become theirs. Our gods are their gods. No wonder trust in man brings a curse.

When we have this mindset, we trust the wrong people, and they hurt us. We trust them because they appear to live up to our ideal. No one can live up to that, so they disappoint us. They are the reason we are in the tomb. We are the reason too. Our ideals demanded that death come. Lying there in that tomb; we want to blame everyone who has hurt us. We have no one to blame but ourselves.

Learning Trust

This entire process brings us into *Jeremiah 17:7, 8 "But blessed is the man who trusts in the Lord, whose confidence is in Him. He will be like a tree planted by the water that sends out its roots by the stream. It does not fear when heat comes; it has no worries in a year of drought and never fails to bear fruit."*

Before, the bride's confidence was in her ideals, her ideas of God. Now lying in the tomb, these are dead, and she is in the first stage of learning to trust God. When she has learned the lessons that come with the tomb and resurrection, she will no longer fear a trial. Drought and difficulty in her life will not throw her because she no longer worships her ideas about God. Instead, she worships only God, and that sustains her during drought. He is the stream next to which He plants her. No longer planted by the streams of men's ideologies, she thrives no matter the circumstances.

Smyrna, the bride, follows the cross and tomb. Smyrna is the opposite of Laodicea. They are poor yet rich. Laodicea is rich, yet poor. Smyrna's doctrine teaches us how to suffer. Laodicea's doctrine teaches us to be proud of our accomplishments and wealth. In fact, wealth often leads to a lukewarm attitude to God. Pride leads us to trust in our gifts, abilities, and plans. The Laodicean church is alive and well in the USA. We have institutionalized self-will and call it God. More about Laodicea later.

Smyrna is actively preparing for the Kingdom. Smyrna knows they are in grinding poverty, but they are doing the will of God. The white robes the bride wears result from righteous acts or obeying God's will. Smyrna will wear these white robes.

Rev. 19:8 'It was given to her to clothe herself in fine linen, bright and clean; for the fine linen is the righteous acts of the saints.'

Smyrna is the opposite of Pergamos and Thyatira, who practiced emperor worship so they could avoid persecution. Emperor worship included feasting in idols temples and fornicating with temple prostitutes. Jews were exempt from emperor worship, but the Jews excluded the Christians and thereby removed their protection from being forced into emperor worship or death. Smyrna had no doctrine of the Nicolaitans as Thyatira did, telling them to compromise with emperor worship.[xiv] Smyrna chooses death rather than compromise. The Lord rebuked Pergamos for swerving from the truth and embracing the doctrines of Balaam and the Nicolaitans. They did this to avoid persecution.

The Lord comes to Smyrna as the one who was dead and is alive. Then He encourages them that if they are faithful unto death, they will receive the crown of life and the second death will not hurt them.

For Reflection

1. Are you compromising to know acceptance, love or get ahead?

2. Will you be faithful to death?

3. Are you ready to lock your garden? If so, write changes you must make.

Prayer

Lover of My Soul help me choose well. I am surrounded by the culture which gives me messages which contradict Your will for me. I fear persecution. Move in my life and make me ready for Your will. I cannot do the work that needs to be done in my heart. I choose faithfulness to You alone.

CHAPTER 7
Pergamos the Worldly Church

The Judicial Christ

Rev. 2:12 "And to the angel of the church in Pergamum, write:
The One who has the sharp two-edged sword says this:"

Here, Christ presents himself as the one who comes for judicial punishment. The word of God and the word He is speaking will judge this church. This sword is small, double-edged and used in close combat.[xv] This is personal to Christ.

Rev. 2:13 'I know where you dwell, where Satan's throne is; and you hold fast My name, and did not deny My faith even in the days of Antipas, My witness, My faithful one, who was killed among you, where Satan dwells.'

14 'But I have a few things against you, because you have there some who hold the teaching of Balaam, who kept teaching Balak to put a stumbling block before the sons of Israel, to eat things sacrificed to idols and to commit acts of immorality. 15 So you also have some who in the same way hold the teaching of the Nicolaitans.'

The Roman emperor worship of the day was to feast and fornicate in idol's temples. Pergamum was a center of emperor worship. This meant Rome expected the Christians to take part. It is possible that the doctrine of the Nicolaitans was to compromise with emperor worship to avoid persecution.[xvi] This is the same worship that caused God to send the Babylonians to kill and take his people captive to Babylon. Judah practiced Baal worship in God's, temple, so the Lord allowed the temple's destruction.

This worship appeals to the flesh. Compromise made sense. It beat dying. This is reasoning without God's Spirit. Often in church history, men compromised rather than stand for God. Those who walked close to His heart like Smyrna did not compromise. The difference is the heart, both the harlot's heart and the bride's heart.

Mystery Babylon set her heart to win the hearts of people. What can they do for her. Will they cooperate with her plan? Their value to her is in how they can help her. Life is about her will.

Mystery Bride focuses on her beloved. She did not start with this focus, for like all humans, her heart wandered during her journey's beginning. But she wanted Him more. He brought a difficulty to her, and she learned to embrace it because it helped her draw close to Him until a single focus on Him became a way of life. She reaches out to people in obedience to His will because He longs to draw them, too. Yet, she does not live for their acceptance. But for His love. She lives for His will.

The Harlot And Babylon

Mystery Babylon includes the way of Balaam. Balaam told Balak the king He could not curse Israel, but if Balak enticed them into Baal worship using the women of Baal, they would curse themselves. Later, Assyria and Babylon took them captive because of Baal worship.

16 'Therefore repent; or else I am coming to you quickly, and I will make war against them with the sword of My mouth.'

The judge will come and pass judgement. The Lord is coming quickly to judge. This Nicolaitan heresy created an emergency in God's eyes. He will use the written word of God and the word he is speaking at that moment. Though called to fidelity to Christ, fear causes compromise. Fear and worship are the same words in Hebrew and Greek. So, fear=worship. So, we worship our ideas because we fear, or we fear God more than we fear persecution. Each is exclusive of the other. We love one and hate the other. Further, embracing emperor worship was hatred toward God.

17 'He who has an ear, let him hear what the Spirit says to the churches.' Hear the plaintive cry of God. "Can you hear me? I died for you to betroth you in love. Can you not overcome the fear of persecution for me?" He carried our sin, for He desires us, and we repay Him with idol worship. So, He cries out, "can you hear me?"

17b 'To him who overcomes,'

To the one who overcomes the false doctrine, to the one who overcomes the idolatry of fear.

His Bride Is Innocent

17c "to him I will give some of the hidden manna, and I will give him a white stone, and a new name written on the stone which no one knows but he who receives it."'

Hidden manna is God's provision of spiritual food xvii and Jesus himself. Only over-comers receive hidden manna. These are mysteries only known in an intimate relationship. The bride and the Bridegroom are a couple and have communication known only them.

The white stone speaks of the bride's innocence and purity. Ancients voted upon guilt or innocence by white and black stones, with black showing guilt. Christ nailed the bride's guilt to the cross. But, to receive this, she must overcome the ways of the harlot. The Lord says she is white, forgiven, innocent by His blood.

He gives her a new name, His name.

Is. 56:5 To them I will give in My house and within My walls a memorial, And a name better than that of sons and daughters; I will give them an everlasting name which will not be cut off.

Note: He gives the new name within the Lord's house. This is the house where He prepares a place for His bride. Further, only one name is better than sons and daughters, and that name is the wife of the Lamb. Only the over-comer will receive this name. It will be a permanent name; everlasting, for she will be His wife for eternity.

For Reflection

1. Will you allow the Lord to judge you with His word and accept what He tells you about the results?

2. Will you choose to surrender?

3. He desires you to enter the love we cannot fully understand,

but we experience. Will you say yes? Write down your reply.

Prayer

Holy One, you are God, and I am not. Help me understand You and Your plan, Your Otherness. Help me choose You and forsake the compromise. Bring me into the Secret Place of Your presence and learn to trust only You.

CHAPTER 8
Thyatira the Idolatrous Church

The Judge

Rev. 2:18 "And to the angel of the church in Thyatira write: The Son of God, who has eyes like a flame of fire, and His feet are like burnished bronze, says this:"

He comes to this church as a judge. What He sees, though they hide it from themselves, will judge them. Calvary tried His feet in the fire. He walked that path to set them free, but most in this church have refused His provision for their sin. He will test His church as He walks among them.

Rev. 2:19 "I know your deeds, and your love and faith and service and perseverance, and that your deeds of late are greater than at first."

This church had deeds of value, love, and faith. Deeds are good, but not always, God led. We work hard for God, but that is not a guarantee He is leading. Because of what follows in this passage, we know some of Thyatira's efforts were not God led.

20'But I have this against you, that you tolerate the woman Jezebel, who calls herself a prophetess, and she teaches and leads My bond-servants astray so that they commit acts of immorality and eat things sacrificed to idols.'

Free will is the genuine believers' most troublesome challenge. Deception cannot influence us if our will is to do God's will. (Jn. 7:17) But our desires often betray us. We do not hear correctly. If we allow the deception that comes with wanting what we want, it can become a way of life. New Testament Jezebel and the Old Testament Jezebel did this.

Jezebel The Harlot

Jezebel, wife of King Ahab, brought Baal worship to Israel. When Babylon took Judah captive, Israel was worshipping Baal in God's temple. (Eze.8) Further, fornication with temple prostitutes and eating meat offered to Baal characterized this worship. Molech was a part of Baal worship with child sacrifice. These idol rites took place in the Lord's temple.

The original Jezebel had 450 prophets of Baal and 400 of Ashtoreth eating at her table. (1Kings 18:19) She executed the prophets of God. (1Kings 18:4) Jezebel had Naboth killed so her husband Ahab could have Naboth's vineyard. (1Kings 21:7-15) She was ruthless, seductive and did anything to get what she demanded.

Jezebel then and now wants to dominate the prophetic in the church. The reason is simple. If you control the prophetic, you can change the minds of the people bit by bit until they are worshipping something besides God, while calling it God. Jezebel does not do this openly. She takes those who are not in the word captive by fake spirituality. Jezebel is adept at looking Godly, but instead it's seduction. Similar to an octopus that camouflages itself with ink, the tentacles of Jezebel grab its prey and will not let go unless someone in authority wields the sword and cuts off the tentacles.

People of God's voice, such as a prophet or pastor, watch out! Jezebel will do her best to dominate these leaders. If she cannot dominate them, she will turn the rest of the church against them. This way, she dominates the prophetic and set herself up as the one in charge. Or she seduces weak pastors and rules through them.

In this 1st century church, the easy way was to compromise. The bronze trade was big in Thyatira. If you were in the "union", they expected you to worship the gods of the union. This included idol's feasts. To quit the union was to abandon your way of providing for your family. Jezebel devised a way to serve the union and Christianity. The problem was her way was idolatry.[xvii]

Pergamos observed Nicolaitan's doctrine, which sounds similar. Both worship idols with cult prostitutes and both eat meat sacrificed to idols but, Baal worship is worse in God's eyes than any other. Equally bad is co-opting the prophetic. Indeed, the Israelites refused God's covenant by His voice in Exodus 19, so He gave them a law they could never keep. Calvary reestablished the covenant by His voice. Jezebel's seduction of his people replaces his covenant voice with her voice. The bride companies are people of God's voice.

Further, the harlot companies are people of the seducing harlots' voice. People once connected to God's voice now depend on Jezebel's. For more on this subject, read *The Veiled Ploy* by the late John Paul Jackson.

Rev.21 'I gave her time to repent, and she does not want to repent of her immorality.' Her deceptive will and doctrines are now an indispensable part of her life and the lives those she entices and deceives. Thyatira is history except for the remnant.

22 'Behold, I will throw her on a bed of sickness, and those who commit adultery with her into great tribulation, unless they repent of her deeds.'

Those who follow her have themselves followed their own will. Certainly, something in her doctrine appeals to them more than what others teach. Those who follow her must repent of "her" deeds. This does not mean they don't have their sinful deeds. But they must repent of accepting Jezebel's influence. Those freed of this influence often need guidance to find their way.

23 'And I will kill her children with pestilence, and all the churches will know that I am He who searches the minds and hearts; and I will give to each one of you according to your deeds'.

Someone threw the Old Testament Jezebel out of a window, and the dogs ate her leaving only her head and hands and feet. 2Ki. 9:34-35. Her head was her evil plans, her hands were her works, and her feet ran to do evil.

The phrase I will give each of you according to your deeds should strike fear in each compromising heart. In fact, without repentance, no grace of God is available to those who follow

Jezebel's doctrine. Grace justifies true believers. They do not get judged by their deeds, but the blood of Christ justifies them.

The Rest in Thyatira

24'But I say to you, the rest who are in Thyatira, who do not hold this teaching, who have not known the deep things of Satan, as they call them — I place no other burden on you. '

Those not holding to this teaching receive no other burden. Think of those who "hold" this teaching. The teaching, they hold to will judge them. The Lord's eyes of fire see the sin.

25'Nevertheless what you have, hold fast until I come. 26'He who overcomes, and he who keeps My deeds until the end, TO HIM I WILL GIVE AUTHORITY OVER THE NATIONS; 27 AND HE SHALL RULE THEM WITH A ROD OF IRON, AS THE VESSELS OF THE POTTER ARE BROKEN TO PIECES, as I also have received authority from My Father.'

Jesus reassures the bride in this church to hold fast until He comes. The harlot holds fast to sin. The bride holds fast to His grace. She overcomes and keeps His deeds until the end. What were His deeds? *John 5:19 "Therefore Jesus answered and was saying to them, Truly, truly, I say to you, the Son can do nothing of Himself, unless it is something He sees the Father doing; for whatever the Father does, these things the Son also does in like manner."* If Jesus calls us to His deeds, He calls us to obey. We don't need a list of do's and don'ts. We must listen and obey. These listeners receive authority over nations just as Christ has authority.

It takes authority to overcome Jezebel. Elijah ran from her. Elisha anointed Jehu as king to kill Jezebel. Jehu had authority Elijah did not have. Many times, Jezebel deceives those in authority or leadership in the church. This opens the people of God to her seduction. It is up to the leaders to stop her. If someone does not stop her, the Jezebel spirit will dominate the church. The faithful can do nothing but leave. [xviii]

Jezebel's Influence

Her followers want their own will. This illustrates Jezebel's influence and heresy in the following: *2 Peter 2:10 "and especially* those who indulge the flesh in its corrupt desires and despise authority."

God does not count it a light thing when His people accept deception rather than the word's authority. Indulging the flesh follows quickly. *"Daring, self-willed,"* Self-will is not only big with Jezebel but those she seduces. Her doctrine appeals to the flesh.

2 Pet. 2:10 "they do not tremble when they revile angelic majesties. Whereas angels who are greater in might and power do not bring a reviling judgment against them before the Lord. 12 But these, like unreasoning animals, born as creatures of instinct to be captured and killed,"

God has not called us to live by instinct and do as we please. Rather, He has established a Kingdom which operates by spiritual principles. Unfortunately, Jezebel invites others to give in to their instincts all the while appearing spiritual.

2Pet. 2:12 "reviling where they have no knowledge, will in the destruction of those creatures also be destroyed, 13 suffering wrong as the wages of doing wrong. They count it a pleasure to revel (weaken by indulgence) in the daytime. Even Godless Romans kept reveling for at night."

The gatherings of the church when worshipping other gods are reveling in God's eyes. This church was so deceived they believed they were serving God.

13"They are stains and blemishes," The Bride has no spot or wrinkle. *"reveling in their deceptions as they carouse with you,"*

They believe they are worshipping God well, but He tells them they are only reveling in deception. In modern parlance, they are partying around their deceptive beliefs and their other gods.

14 "having eyes full of adultery that never cease from sin," Adultery against God is the way of Jezebel, the way of deception. Sin follows. Even the Pharisees who appeared to have it together were committing adultery with the extra rules they added to the word. They worshipped a God who little resembled Jehovah.

*14b "enticing unstable souls, having a heart trained in **greed, accursed children; 15 forsaking the right way, they have gone astray, having followed the way of Balaam, the son of Beor, who*** *loved the wages of unrighteousness; 16 but he received a rebuke for his own transgression, for a mute donkey, speaking with a voice of a man, restrained the madness of the prophet."*

Balaam told Balak the King that he could not curse Israel, but Baal could lead Israel astray. This is the same sin Jezebel brings to the church. (Numb. 31:16) Compromise is not good for us, it leads us away from God.

2Pet. 2:17 "These are springs without water," Not fulfilling their purpose for existing. No refreshing, no life without water. *"and mists driven by a storm, for whom the black darkness has been reserved."* Driven by a demonic storm. 18 *"For speaking out arrogant words of vanity."* Vanity means empty or futile. This means nothing of value.

1Pet. 1:18 "knowing that you were not redeemed with perishable things like silver or gold from your futile way of life inherited from your forefathers,"

We inherited a futile way of life. Without freedom from this life we speak empty words often, and winds of doctrine can take us captive. *"They entice by fleshly desires, by sensuality, those who barely escape from the ones who live in error,*

19 "promising them freedom while they themselves are slaves (doulas[xix])*of corruption; for by what a man is overcome, by this he is enslaved."* He serves or is enslaved by _____. We are to be the Lord's douloo or slave.

Rev. 2:28 'and I will give him the morning star. 29He who has an ear, let him hear what the Spirit says to the churches.' Jesus is the morning star. The bride has an ear. She rejoices in hearing His voice. The voices of others who are not listening to Him hold no appeal to her. She is seeking the one who is Bridegroom, King, and Judge.

For Reflection

1. Are you open to God's Spirit convicting you of idolatry? When did you last allow this?

2. Do you compromise to avoid persecution? What will you do about it?

3. How can you give yourself as a slave to Christ?

Prayer

Lord, your kingdom includes the things my flesh fights. Help me live by Your Spirit rather than my flesh. Let me hear your convicting voice and embrace Your will.

CHAPTER 9
Sardis The Dead Church

Rev. 3:1 "To the angel of the church in Sardis write: He who has the seven Spirits of God and the seven stars, says this: 'I know your deeds, that you have a name that you are alive, but you are dead.'"

Notice first who is speaking. It is He who holds the seven Spirits of God and the seven stars. Prior descriptions show us the one speaking is the Lord himself, who was dead and is alive forever.

This church is in trouble. They received no commendation in the Lord's opening statement, but a strong censure. Their reputation said one thing and their lives speak the truth.

The Seven Spirits

Rev. 1:4 "John to the seven churches that are in Asia: Grace to you and peace, from Him who is and who was and who is to come, and from the seven Spirits who are before His throne, 5 and from Jesus Christ, the faithful witness, the firstborn of the dead, and the ruler of the kings of the earth."

The Seven Spirits are the Holy Spirit, and we see the Seven Spirits in the furnishings of the temple and tabernacle. (Ex 37:17) They are in heaven before his throne and in Zechariah's vision.

*Zech. 4:2 'He said to me, "What do you see?" And I said, "I see, and behold, a lampstand all of gold with its bowl on the top of it, and its seven lamps on it with seven spouts belonging to each of the **lamps which are on the top of it 3 also two olive trees by it, one on the right side of the bowl and the other on its left side."** 4' Then I said to the angel who was speaking with me saying, "What are these, my lord?'5 'So the angel who was speaking with me answered and said*

to me, "Do you not know what these are?" And I said, "No, my lord."
6 Then he said to me, "This is the word of the LORD to Zerubbabel
saying, 'Not by might nor by power, but by My Spirit,' says the LORD of
hosts."'

God granted this vision to Zerubbabel to let him know the task
the Lord assigned him; Zerubbabel would finish by the power and
might of God, not by his strength. God showed him a lampstand
with seven lights. This lamp-stand is a type of the multiplicity of
working of the Spirit of God. In Revelation, our Bridegroom holds
this lamp stand that searches our hearts and reveals our thoughts
and deeds.

The book of Revelation is Jesus Christ's revelation and His
bride's unveiling. History is for His sake, and the mystery of the
bride. He holds everything in His hand. He created not only the
planet on which we live, but He created us for himself. We lose
sight of this to our peril. Unfortunately, most of the Sardis church
lost sight of this truth. As a result, the Judge said they were dead.

Alive or Dead

The church of Sardis believed they were alive. Possibly they had
rousing praise services and marvelous liturgies. These were their
actual deeds, which the Creator Lamb knows. Their deeds gave
them a reputation with a man, but God said they were dead.
The nature of deception is that you may believe one thing about
yourself, however, another thing, possibly an opposite thing, is
true. Hypocrisy or play-acting gave them a reputation for being
alive. To those not tuned in to the Holy Spirit, they may look holy.
But their deeds were not obedient to God's voice.

Churches do this today, as well. They are skilled at looking
alive, "you have a name that you are alive," but the focus is not
on loving and knowing Christ and making Him known to others.
Jesus told the Pharisees that they made their converts twice
the sons of hell as themselves *(Mt.23)*. However, the Pharisees
thought they were the enlightened ones. The people followed
them and held them in high honor.

Even our efforts to bring people into the "church" could bring them into a dead, play-acting church with a reputation for life, but not the life of God. Often, dead religion resembles the relationship with Christ because of our worship of traditions in God's place.

We see the standard by which we must and should measure in the Ten Commandments and then restated by Christ himself.

Mark 12:29 "The most important one," answered Jesus, "is this: 'Hear, O Israel, the Lord our God, the Lord is one. 30 Love the Lord your God with all your heart and with all your soul and with all your mind and with all your strength.' 31 The second is this: 'Love your neighbor as yourself.' There is no commandment greater than these."

We can build large churches, lead great programs, do many admirable works, but, that does not qualify us in God's eyes. Do we love Him with everything within us? Do we seek Him to know Him or for His stuff? If we don't take time with Him, do we miss Him? Does our heart ache for more time with Him? Is He number one in our lives?

Spiritual death parallels the life of a star. If a star dies in the sky, it takes scores of years for that death to become evident because of the speed at which light travels and our distance from the star. It takes time for spiritual death to become manifest to the casual observer, but the King of Kings knows the truth because He is the Righteous Judge, and He sees what others cannot. The same is true of dead churches. It is a time before the death manifests to the eye of the beholder because the culture in that church accepts death as life.

God, in His mercy, confronts us as He did the Sardis church. He knows if the life we demonstrate is His life or man's idea of life. Will we listen when He sends others to tell us we have a problem? Will we listen to Him?

But there was hope for Sardis. *Rev. 3:2 'Wake up, and strengthen the things that remain, which were about to die; for I have not found your deeds completed in the sight of My God. 'The One who holds the seven stars'* (the seven churches, Rev. 1:19) says, *'wake up'*. This is a call to set aside apathy, self-will, and self-satisfaction.

Idols and Images

In the American church, we worship many mental images. Namely, the gods of comfort, convenience, mammon, and individualism are major among them. As we worship these, we convince ourselves that we worship only Him. So, we rationalize our dedication to our mental images. They are so much a part of us they appear normal. This is hypocrisy in His eyes.

Even without our cultural idols, we bow down to mental idols from our formative years because of the futile (empty) way of life we experienced growing up in our families. In addition, every country's culture and every family culture worship idols. These stand in the way of our seeing Him as He is.

Hypocrisy keeps us from seeing the idols, from seeing we are dying as concerns true faith and love for the Lord. The wider culture and often the church culture keep us from seeing we are practicing dead religion instead of the life of God to which He invites us.

Something was still alive in Sardis and the American church. Undeniably, the faithful core, the remnant refuses to bow the knee to the gods of this world. This remnant forsakes the family and cultural idolatry. Similarly, this remnant hears the messengers God sends. They listen to His voice in the Secret Place and search His word, see their idolatry, and repent. The Glory of God addresses himself to this remnant to wake up and strengthen what remains before it too dies.

This remnant speaks forth the truth to the rest of the assembly to help waken them to love again. Often, the assembly wounds the remnant over-comers for the message, but the over-comer continues on his path. This is the pattern shown in the Prophets and Psalms.

The deeds of Sardis were not complete. This could mean many things, but likely it included participation in spiritual adultery, (James 4:4) rather than wholehearted devotion to Christ. It means life sidetracked them from God's purposes.

Rev. 3:3 'So remember what you have received and heard; and keep it and repent. Therefore, if you do not wake up, I will come like a thief, and you will not know at what hour I will come to you.'

Remember means to mention or discuss. To remember, we recite what we need to remember. Likewise, we should recount the things God has taught us. Then go back to early lessons and deeds of God and repeat them out loud. We must repeat the scriptural lessons He taught us in the Secret Place. These lessons set us free from the futility of our formative years. If we forget the lessons, we embrace futility again. Deception captures our minds and keeps us from the truth and freedom we find in the Secret Place of His presence.

The Judge tells us to keep what we received. This means to guard it. In fact, we are to set a sentry around the things that God taught us every hour of every day. We cannot do this apart from His help. We find His help in His presence. If we are not seeking Him, we will use the gifts and graces He has given to us, so we can build a following, a life or a work that looks alive.

What did they receive that they needed to keep or guard it (obey NIV)? Christ redeemed them, *1 Pet.1:19 "with precious blood, as of a lamb unblemished and spotless, the blood of Christ"* God gave something better than gold, and the honor and acceptance that gold can buy, for each member of the bride. The bridal price paid by the Bridegroom Lamb to enter a consummated relationship was His blood.

Sardis was not obedient to God's voice. Further, they did not remember the terrible sacrifice made on their behalf. The world's promises of riches, satisfaction, or honor captured them. Sardis was sleeping when they should be awake and doing His will.

The Son of God did the Father's will. *(Jn. 4:1, 8:28, 12:49)* He calls us to his will.

We speak of being transformed into His image, but what does that mean? How can we measure this? These passages give us a clue.

John 5:19 'Therefore Jesus answered and was saying to them, Truly, truly, I say to you, the Son can do nothing of Himself, unless it is something He sees the Father doing; for whatever the Father does, these things the Son also does in like manner."

Jn. 17:4 "I glorified You on the earth, having accomplished the work which You have given Me to do."

Jn. 14:10 "Do you not believe that I am in the Father, and the Father is in Me? The words that I say to you I do not speak on My own initiative, but the Father abiding in Me does His works."

John 14: 24 "He who does not love Me does not keep My words; and the word which you hear is not Mine, but the Father's who sent Me."

The Father spoke to and through Jesus. He sent the Holy Spirit to speak to and through us. Jesus did the will of the Father. Further, he spoke as the Father spoke. We become like Jesus by beholding Him. He was obedient unto death.

Beholding His death helps us carry our cross. In the meantime, we will search out His perfect obedience and perfect love as the measure of our lives. It is something we will never obtain in this life, but with our focus on Him, we will make progress.

He admonishes Sardis to strengthen the little that remains before it dies, or they will miss the time of His visitation. This is a serious consequence for their lethargy. Indeed, this chastisement is one of the most serious admonitions he gives to those who claim his name.

Overcomers

Rev. 3: 4 'But you have a few people in Sardis who have not soiled their garments; and they will walk with Me in white, for they are worthy. 5 He who overcomes will thus be clothed in white garments: and I will not erase his name from the book of life, and I will confess his name before My Father and before His angels. 6 He who has an ear, let him hear what the Spirit says to the churches.'

Few have not soiled their clothes. This means that the rest have soiled their clothes. There is the remnant, (Ezra 9:8, Is.10:20-22, Mic. 5:7-8, Rom. 11:5), the over-comers within the church. These are the bride. A study of the Old Testament shows God is calling those who name Him, but only a remnant of that called people will hear His call to the bride. Moreover, the remnant bride will walk with him dressed in white. *(For more on the remnant see Micah 4-5, Zeph. 3:13, Zech. 8:11, Rom 9:27, Rom 11:5)*

Over-comers dress in white. An over-comer is the ready bride.

So, who are the over-comers? They are those who commit to the process of being redeemed from the futile life handed down to them and, likewise, who have allowed His grace to permeate their mess and set them free to be completely His. Further, over-comers are finding victory over the idols and lies of this life. They are not perfect, but they know God is their source. Over-comers surrender to Him and make Him Lord of All.

This is a notable accomplishment because the process is painful. It requires us dying to our will and becoming alive to His will. *Phil. 3:7 "But whatever was to my profit I now consider loss for the sake of Christ.8 What is more, I consider everything a loss compared to the surpassing greatness of knowing Christ Jesus my Lord, for whose sake I have lost all things. I consider them rubbish that I may gain Christ."*

An over-comer *"counts **everything** a loss for the sake of **knowing Christ Jesus my Lord**"*, Phil 3:8 (emphasis mine). Their treasure is not an earthly treasure. They have overcome their love of the world's offerings. In fact, their treasure is in Him alone, knowing Him, loving Him and holding Him most precious. An over-comer wears white, with unsoiled clothes and God calls them worthy. What makes them worthy of wearing white? The answer is obedience.

"Remember what you have heard: obey it and repent." NIV.

What did they hear? He redeemed and called them to an intimate relationship. Most of the Sardis church forgot their call to be His bride. They forgot to live in close relationship with Him. Sadly, this describes much of today's church. There is much activity, but little intimacy.

For Reflection

1. Are you obedient to the voice and direction of God? If not, what keeps you from obedience? Confess this to Him and commit to His Lordship.

2. Do you worship with people who seem alive, but are dead? If so, ask the Lord if He wants you to continue with them. Are you a voice to them or are you to stay to pray for them? How can you

keep intimacy alive with Jesus while there?

3. Do you remember what you have heard? Then obey it and repent and come back to the one who stands ready to receive you.

Prayer

Terrifying Judge, Merciful Savior, hear my prayer and forgive me for the futile ways I follow and the idols I serve. Set me free and make me wholly yours. I want to learn who you are. Draw me into your awesome presence, so I learn to live for You and to live in Your presence.

CHAPTER 10
Philadelphia the Ready Bride
His Bride

God gave the book of Revelation to His bride so she will be ready for the Bridegroom. Its purpose is so she might fulfill the deepest yearning of His ravished heart. Revelation 21 gives us an extraordinary picture of His bride. Note that at the end of the book of Revelation, He showcases His bride; Revelation tells us that story, so the bride becomes ready, and the Bridegroom comes forth.

The letters to the churches are a specific admonition to His bride, so she knows how to be ready. When He speaks to the next church, the church of Philadelphia, He speaks of the New Jerusalem coming down out of heaven from God. *(Rev. 3:12)* This city is the bride of Revelation 21. The Bridegroom is speaking to His bride when He speaks to Philadelphia. The church or believer that has the characteristics of the Philadelphia church is the bride.

Rev. 3:7 "And to the angel of the church in Philadelphia write: He who is holy, who is true, who has the key of David, who opens, and no one will shut, and who shuts, and no one opens, says this:"

The name Philadelphia means brotherly love[xx]. [xxi] Christ exhibited this when He died for us and we see this exemplified in this Philadelphia church. This means we show love one for another because of our intimate relationship with Him.

The Lord's church is fragmented one from the other, but the love He calls us to reach way beyond our love for our brothers in the Spirit with whom we agree. We are to love and lay our lives down for others in our world to bring them to Christ. We are to love sacrificially those who name His name even when we have differences in doctrine.

Are we willing to take up our cross daily and die to our ideas of life and become alive to His will? Will we place our focus on Him or be distracted by what looks spiritual? Regarding this, will we buy into the world's ideas of "church"?

Years ago, many purchased jewelry that said WWJD, or ("What would Jesus do?"). This phrase was on lanyards, purse and backpack straps, key chains and myriads of other things. It was a slogan, but few asked the question of themselves seriously. If we had asked that question, the love of God for the hurting would transform entire communities, the poor and marginalized. Jesus lived a life of self-giving and obedience to the Father. If we followed Him, the world could not resist His love. What **would** Jesus do?

He tells us He has the key of David, and what He opens no one can shut. *Is. 22:22* speaks this phrase of Messiah. *"The key to the house of David"* is the wording in the Isaiah passage. Jesus was from David's line as regards His humanity. He is of the line of Israel's kings and is the King of Kings.

Moreover, He has authority to shut and open doors. For those who are faithful, who love Him with their whole heart and do not serve other gods, He will open doors that man or evil entity cannot shut. Much of the church wants certain doors open but not, other doors. The Philadelphia church is an obedient church and they wait upon the open doors He has for them. They allow His will to become their will.

He can close doors, so no one opens them. This comforts those who choose His will. He keeps evil at bay and work circumstances toward good. (Romans 8: 18-20.)

Rom. 8:20 "For the creation was subjected to futility, not willingly, but because of Him who subjected it, in hope 21 that the creation itself also will be set free from its slavery to corruption into the freedom of the glory of the children of God."

This passage shows He allows suffering to set us free from the futility of our upbringing and our choices. We should see this as a promise for our good, but we often run from this truth. We do this by trying to control our destiny as we evade His will for our own will. In fact, the Philadelphia Church does not fit into this mold. This church is faithful.

Rev. 3:8 'I know your deeds. Behold, I have put before you an open door which no one can shut, because you have a little power, and have kept My word, and have not denied My name.'

He knows the deeds of the Philadelphia church. Because of their deeds, He has set before them an open door that cannot be shut. They have a little strength because they are a tiny community[xxii] compared to the other churches. We see that small group again, the remnant. Though the other churches have a remnant within them; this small church **is** a remnant.

They are faithful and have kept His word. Think of it this way. God wrote Revelation to the bride, so she may know the Bridegroom's plan in the last day. He wrote it, so she will understand her calling to God and ministry. She is the bride of Revelation 21. The remnant is the bride. Similarly, the Philadelphia church is the bride. The bride is in dying churches. She hears His voice.as she is amid the dying church; she rises above that death by hearing His voice. Then, she takes a stand for His heart in that place and guards her heart from the death that surrounds her. Willingly, she stands alone amid the surrounding culture. Yet she is not alone, for she is His.

He is her comfort when those who reject His presence reject her. She finds His presence in the Secret Place when not manifest in her church. The bride takes up her cross daily and, in love and obedience, carries it knowing the smile of His face is enough.

Because the bride has learned to listen to the voice of her Beloved, she sees the word of God through His heart. Moreover, the word of God is her life and breath as His Spirit breathes on it. She listens for His voice continuously, understanding that His voice alone sustains her and change her into His image. Like the Psalmist David, she says, *"I will see Your face in righteousness; I shall be satisfied when I awake in Your likeness." Ps.17:15 NKJV.* Nothing short of this can hold her.

This bride has not denied His name. In the Old Testament

times the name included character, authority and function. This was also true of the gods of the nations, including the Israelite God. Character, authority and function help the worshipper understand how to worship properly. The ensuing passages illustrate proper worship:

Deut. 6:5 "You shall love the LORD your God with all your heart and with all your soul and with all your might." Idolatry defiles and denies His name.

Phil 2:9 "For this reason also, God highly exalted Him, and bestowed on Him the name which is above every name,

10 "so that at the name of Jesus EVERY KNEE WILL BOW, of those who are in heaven and on earth and under the earth,

11 "and that every tongue will confess that Jesus Christ is Lord, to the glory of God the Father."

Phil. 2:9-11 is our heritage as his bride. We will see everyone who denied his name confess he is Lord.

The next section is a contrast to earlier passages. *Jer. 7:30 "For the sons of Judah have done that which is evil in My sight, declares the LORD, they have set their detestable things in the house which is called by My name, to defile it."* Two reasons God calls this evil in His eyes is because this action denies His name and is carried out in His house, in the place of His presence. In other words, adultery against Him takes place in front of Him. Philadelphia does not indulge in this. This church is faithful to keep her eyes on the Lord. This does not characterize the whole church.

He calls us by His name. Consider Jeremiah. *Jer. 15:16 "Your words were found, and I ate them, And Your words became for me a joy and the delight of my heart; For I have been called by Your name, O LORD, God of hosts. "*

As the Lord's bride, He calls us by His name. Idolatry profanes His name. Idolatry is adultery since we are His bride. But Jeremiah guarded his heart by eating, by devouring the words of God. The Lord's words were Jeremiah's delight. So, what is that name we should honor and embrace?

Jere. 16:21 "Therefore behold, I am going to make them know — This time I will make them know My power and My might; And they *shall know that My name is **the LORD**."*

*Jere. 31:35 "This is what the LORD says, he who appoints the sun to shine by day, who decrees the moon and stars to shine by night, who stirs up the sea so that its waves roar **the LORD Almighty** is his name."*

*"Jere. 33:2 "Thus says the LORD who made the earth, the LORD who formed it to establish it, **the LORD** is His name,"*

*Jere. 33:16 "In those days Judah will be saved and Jerusalem will dwell in safety; and this is the name by which she will be called: **the LORD is our righteousness**."*

There are many scriptures that give other names for him. One truth we can gain from these scriptures is that he is Lord. Since no Lord is greater than Lord God Almighty, we are to lay aside everything that grips our hearts to receive Him alone.

Rev. 3:9 "Behold, I will cause those of the synagogue of Satan, who say that they are Jews and are not, but lie — I will make them come and bow down at your feet, and make them . know, that I have loved you."

The synagogue of Satan here is likely those Jews that persecuted the Christians. This occurred in Smyrna and Philadelphia.[xxiii] Moreover, as the Philadelphia church endured the persecution, the day will come when those who persecuted the church will recognize that the Lord loves His church. This is true of those who persecute the bride today.

Rev. 3:10 "Because you have kept the word of My perseverance, I also will keep you from the hour of testing, that hour which is about to come upon the whole world, to test those who dwell on the earth. "

Because of the Philadelphia church's faithful endurance, He keeps them from the hour of trial that will come on the entire earth. Some think this means the church will be gone during the tribulation. Only God knows if this is true. One thing we understand is that the Lord keeps those who love Him above everything else. He hides them in the Secret Place of His presence. He reserves the Secret Place for His beloved bride. The reason is that she is the only one who cares to seek Him there.

Rev 3:11 'I am coming quickly; hold fast what you have, so that no one will take your crown.'

He tells those who read the book of Revelation to hold on to what you have. Hold on no matter what others say to you. When you keep the word of the Lord and do not deny His name, He has crowns stored up for you.

Two crowns are the crown of glory and the crown of life, *(James 1:12 and 1 Pet. 5:4)*. Don't let the enemy steal your crowns by deceit and the many "isms" and people he uses to spread his deceit. Further, remember who you are and whose you are. If the bride stays connected to Him, no one will take her crowns. She will have them to cast at His feet in worship for eternity.

Rev. 3:12 'He who overcomes, I will make him a pillar in the temple of My God, and he will not go out from it anymore;' This is an amazing promise to those who hunger for Him and His presence. His beloved bride yearns for Him. He is her strength, her everything while on earth, and she will live in His presence forever. There is no greater reward.

The word overcomes is the word Nikao[xxiv] in the Greek, meaning to conquer. The one who conquers the idolatry and the evil presence behind idolatry is an over-comer. Because the bride is uncertain which voice is His, she runs to Him. She waits until He makes Himself and His truth known to her. Then the bride overcomes by His word spoken by His Spirit in His presence. She does not rely on her natural gifts of study alone. Many study without His Spirit because they study with another motive than to know Him, such as to impress men. Thus, their wrong motive deceives them. His bride knows only His Spirit can enlighten the scriptures, so she knows what He desires. She does not study so she can have knowledge and impress men. The bride studies so she will know Him and satisfy His heart with her love. She cries out to Him, and the cry of her heart is something like this:

Blazing Glory

Blazing Glory, just His blazing glory
I would see.
Just to fall at His feet as dead,
this I must be.

Dead to all, alive to Him,
dross burned out along with sin.
Blazing Glory is what I need
to destroy the weed and the seed
of iniquity in my heart.

Blazing Glory, burning fire
Purging, consuming all other desires.
God formed in me, Christ within
shining forth, convicting of sin.

Blazing Glory,
God!
I must see!!!
Deal with the sin that dwells in me!
Visit me now. Hear my heart cry!
Visit me now, Lord Most High!

Blazing Glory, my only Lord
Make my heart agree with your's.
You who sit in Blazing Glory come now
this one at your feet must bow.

That Blazing Glory through me will show,
and cause others to want to know.
Purify me Oh, Blazing Light,
dissipate darkness, no more night.

Blazing Glory come now come
I wait upon You my heart is numb.
But awake, alive, revived I will be,
when Blazing Glory shines through me.

Are you refined to purity yet? If not, God's fire is at hand, jump in.

Rev. 3:12b "and I will write on him the name of My God, and the name of the city of My God, the new Jerusalem, which comes down out of heaven from My God, and My new name." This is a bridal statement. Rev. 19 and 21 show us this city is the bride ready for her husband.

Jeremiah's Challenge

Consider Jeremiah, who carried the bride's faithful heart. When God called him, he was young. Jeremiah did not recognize the cost of the Prophet's call. Jeremiah in chapter 20, beginning in verse 1 prophesies against the temple. Because of this, a priest higher in rank than Him has Him beaten and put in stocks. This is public humiliation for doing God's will. He expresses his disillusionment in the next scripture.

Jer. 20:7 "O LORD, You have deceived me, and I was deceived; You have overcome me and prevailed. "

Jeremiah cries out to God that the Lord overcame him the same way an older man takes advantage of a younger woman. He did not expect this depth of rejection, shame, and loneliness. But he bears the Lord's name. In fact, he must answer the Lord's call to prophesy the nation's destruction, even though he is a tenderhearted man. His call fights against his own nature. People will reject him as he obeys and speaks.

God himself made Jeremiah a tenderhearted man, yet the Lord expects and anoints Jeremiah to speak of the unimaginable destruction of the people of God. As Jeremiah obeys, he cries out.

"I never knew it could get this bad. You said you would be with me when you called me. I did not bargain for this. You withheld this information from me." It is one thing to have such a difficult message. It is another experiencing rejection by everyone because of the message. "You deceived me; you wooed me and deceived me."

God's call to Jeremiah in chapter 1 did not prepare his tender heart for the depth of rejection he was to receive. God does not reveal the whole story of our lives to us when we begin our calling. He tells us to count the cost. But sometimes we cannot read the small print because we are not far enough along to understand what the call and obedience to the call entail.

Over time, God instructed Jeremiah not to marry or attend funerals or celebrations (Jer. 16). Others threw him in a pit, beat and rejected him. The Lord was his comfort, and sometimes that was not enough. It was then he had to remember he bore the Lord's name. He, like so many of us, faced unbearable pain and a choice. Should he walk away from the call and from God? For Jeremiahs of this world, that is no choice. With the heart of the bride beating in his chest, he must continue to follow as the cost plays out. Returning to life without God is unthinkable.

The consolation is that he does not pay that cost alone and neither do we. Because of one who paid the supreme penalty and in Jeremiah's day and ours, those who sought the Lord with all their hearts will find him *(Jer. 29:12)*.

Now we understand more what this means because through Christ we see the bride revealed. Yet Jeremiah found in the Lord alone his hiding place. God called Jeremiah by his name. The ah in his name is the same as Yah. Yah means "I Am." "I am everything you need now or in the future." He answers every yearning in I Am if we will allow it.

One of Jeremiah's mistakes was that he assumed things when God called him. Jeremiah assumed the call would be easier and more affirming than it was. He did not know God well yet. Jeremiah needed to become an over-comer even as we do. He must overcome the persecution without blaming God for the persecution. When he blamed God, he did so because he did not yet understand the Lord's heart well.

Our Endurance
Similar to Jeremiah, the pain we endure is a token of what men did to the Lord, the Husband of Israel. Until we understand this, we will struggle with blaming God. We cannot understand this apart from the Lord revealing His heart to us in the Secret Place. We, like Jeremiah, must overcome our expectations of how this life in God works.

Further, we must submit to God and trust His heart, no matter our circumstances. Overcoming at this level is difficult work. But the Lord himself was Jeremiah's portion and consolation when He allowed him to be. The same is true for us. Today the following scriptures are part of our consolation along with the Lord himself.

Rev. 21:9 'Then one of the seven angels who had the seven bowls full of the seven last plagues came and spoke with me, saying, 'Come here, I will show you the bride, the wife of the Lamb.' 10 And he carried me away in the Spirit to a great and high mountain, and showed me the holy city, Jerusalem, coming down out of heaven from God, 11 having the glory of God. Her brilliance was like a very costly stone, as a stone of crystal-clear jasper."'

She is being prepared as a bride for her Husband. The bride is New Jerusalem. We will live in His presence forever.

Rev 22:4 "they will see His face, and His name will be on their foreheads.

The bride's satisfaction comes when she sees His face and is beholding Him through eternity. He calls her by His name. He inscribes His name on her forever.

Rev. 3:13 'He who has an ear, let him hear what the Spirit says to the churches.' Are we listening? For what are we listening? Is it the world's or the majority's voice, our truth, or are we listening for His voice? *"He who has an ear let him hear..."* Jeremiah paid the price to hear. It was the price of rejection and the wounding of His tender heart. The least price we must pay to listen is to surrender our idols and everything dear to us. Are we listening? To the one who is listening, our Bridegroom says, *"let him hear"*

For Reflection

1. Do you feel as if God deceived you? Are you struggling with bitterness against Him? If you do, journal what He says to you about this problem? Give Him time to give you the entire answer. Sometimes we are not ready to hear what He says even though we believe we are. Other layers of deception may need removal first.

2. Are you keeping the word of the Lord? This means keeping His written word and what He has spoken to you.

3. Have you in any way denied His name? Does the way you live your life deny Him?

4. What things do you need to overcome or conquer?

Prayer

Lord, help me keep your word and obey your voice. I live in ways that do not glorify You. Sometimes I am overcome by sin rather than overcoming sin. I want to be ready for our wedding. Show me Your unbridled holiness and Your unfathomable love.

CHAPTER 11
The Church That Thinks They Are Ready

Rev. 3:14 "To the angel of the church in Laodicea write:15 'I know your deeds, that you are neither cold nor hot; I wish that you were cold or hot. 16 So because you are lukewarm, and neither hot nor cold, I will spit you out of My mouth. 17 Because you say, "I am rich, and have become wealthy, and have need of nothing," and you do not know that you are wretched and miserable and poor and blind and naked, 18 I advise you to buy from Me gold refined by fire so that you may become rich, and white garments so that you may clothe yourself, and that the shame of your nakedness will not be revealed; and eye salve to anoint your eyes so that you may see.'"

Laodicea's Arrogance

This letter has a pointed admonition. The back-story to this city is that it had a textile industry that produced shiny black wool, an eye salve industry and they were rich.

Like the developed nations of our day, this church lived in an area of great wealth. This wealth influenced the Laodicean church. The culture the wealth created was influencing the church rather than the church changing the culture. The result was their love for God was lukewarm, like their water supply that started cold and hot but was lukewarm when it got to their city.[xxv]

God speaks to those things in which they were self-sufficient. Laodicea said they needed nothing yet; they were *"wretched and miserable, poor, blind and naked. "* Their hearts deceived them. Though they were rich and self-sufficient according to worldly standards, they were not rich by the Lord's standards. Their pursuit of wealth kept them from seeing they were poor. They were oblivious to the truth that they were no longer pursuing Him with red-hot love. The ritual of church attendance and good works were devoid of true devotion. Perhaps, like much of the church in the developed nations, you could "give your life to Jesus" and not "carry your cross."

Rev. 3: 19 'Those whom I love, I reprove and discipline; therefore, be zealous and repent.'

He was letting them know, letting today's Laodicean church know, He only comes to confront us because He loves us. In His love, He calls us to repentance. We are to repent of the belief, that we can see though we are blind, we are clothed though we are naked; we are rich though we are poor.

How can His church have these problems? It is a matter of focus. Deception blinds and deceives, so we cannot tell we are blind. When our focus is on the wrong things, over time, we lose the ability to recognize his truth. If we choose our way more than His glorious presence and way, we can easily accept a counterfeit that feels good to us. Rather, we accept what our itching ears and wandering heart want to hear.

This means His presence may no longer be in our assemblies, but we have accepted the goosebumps of a counterfeit in place of His abiding presence. In the USA, we live in an entertainment culture and are exporting this culture worldwide. Since we become like that which we behold with reverence, over time, what we view often has the power to change our perspective.

Further, Westerners have felt goosebumps or tears when a movie or performance is particularly good. We do this in church, as well. We judge whether we have God's presence by criteria that often has nothing to do with His presence.

This is performance-based religion's role. For example, if we believe we must perform to receive the love we will seek an objective standard on which to measure our service. We find many outward measures the world, the flesh and the devil approve. Perhaps we measure our fervor by dressing a certain way. It would be difficult to hear God say that was not the measure He uses.

We could believe if we dress this way, we are in good standing.

We trust that what we do for works of service or obedience to the letter of the law is what He wants. We do this even though we argue that He justifies us through His blood alone and our faith in His blood alone. Our words say one thing, and our lives shout another. But we cannot hear the shout of God because of deception. The problem with deception is that we do not know our deception unless we cry out for truth.

Rev. 3:20 "Behold, I stand at the door and knock; if anyone hears My voice and opens the door, I will come into him and will dine with him, and he with Me."

Why Is God Knocking

He is knocking on the door of His church. What a sad commentary on the end-time church and many churches throughout the ages. When we live with abundance, we tend to shut Him out. Why not? We can do this Christian thing ourselves. Of course, we do not think this consciously. But gradually we are working our program, and we shut Him out, knocking. Can you see the tears in His eyes as He knocks? He knocks and then speaks *"if anyone hears my voice, and opens the door."* The Bridegroom Lamb is shut out knocking and asking us to open the door. Since our deception and arrogance are great in the Laodicean church, we cannot hear his plea.

He knocks on the door of congregations and of individuals. Many will never hear.

Rev. 3:21 "He who overcomes, I will grant to him to sit down with Me on My throne, as I also overcame and sat down with My Father on His throne."

We must conquer the enemy's deceit, the futile way of life handed down from our forefathers and the idolatry that comes with that futility. Also, we have to conquer the fears and arrogance that cause us to worship false gods. Another enemy of truth is the cousin to fear, the disobedience that arises out of our fear. Likewise, we need to overcome our self-sufficiency and ability to work this ourselves. And most of all, we should open the door to Him, so He can fellowship with us and show us our deception.

Rev. 3:22 "He who has an ear, let him hear what the Spirit says to the churches."

Can We Hear

Again, He asks if we hear him. Our inability to hear is a serious problem and locks Him out of our assemblies and leaves Him knocking on the door of His church. Open the door, and He will come in and commune with us and us with Him. Then revival will take place.

"Can you hear Me now?" He cries out. "If you can hear, listen. The Spirit is speaking."

He offers freedom from futility, freedom from the temporal and fullness of relationship with the Lamb who redeemed us if we will listen and obey.

Rev. 16:15 "Behold, I am coming like a thief. Blessed is the one who stays awake and keeps his clothes, so that he will not walk about naked and men will not see his shame."

Blessed is He who buys from Him gold refined in the fire, white robes (to cover His nakedness) and eyes salve that he may see. We cannot, by our cleverness or much acting, produce these things. Rather, they only come from His hand. Everything we produce in our effort is a counterfeit. Will He find us naked?

For Reflection

1. Are you worshipping the gods of the Laodicean culture around you? Name them. These gods could be pride, deception, money or mammon, spiritual blindness, self-righteousness, fear of exposure, and others. What scriptures can take these gods captive?

PRAYER

Lord help! The Laodicean culture around me influences me. I worship various idols. Help me get free from them all. Show me how to take the thoughts captive that allow these idols to reign in my life. Show me the scriptures I need to stand in to get victory over these idols.

PART THREE
Judgment of The Harlot
Chapter 12

Her Smoke Rises Up

Rev. 17:1 'Then one of the seven angels who had the seven bowls came and spoke with me, saying, "Come here, I will show you the judgment of the great harlot who sits on many **waters, 2 with whom the kings of the earth committed acts of immorality, and those who dwell on the earth were made drunk with the wine of her immorality."** *3And he carried me away in the Spirit into a wilderness; and I saw a woman sitting on a scarlet beast, full of blasphemous names, having seven heads and ten horns. 4 The woman was clothed in purple and scarlet, and adorned with gold and precious stones and pearls, having in her hand a gold cup full of abominations and of the unclean things of her immorality, 5 and on her forehead a name was written, a mystery, "BABYLON THE GREAT, THE MOTHER OF HARLOTS AND OF THE ABOMINATIONS OF THE EARTH."* *And I saw the woman drunk with the blood of the saints, and with the blood of the witnesses of Jesus. When I saw her, I wondered greatly? 7 And the angel said to me, "Why do you wonder? I will tell you the mystery of the woman and of the beast that carries her, which has the seven heads and the ten horns.'*

Judgment Time

The harlot sits on waters, kings and a beast since she is an economic and religious system. In our understanding, the false bride is in her. The waters are people; the kings are kings throughout history and the beast upon which she rides will destroy her. *Rev. 17:9-18:8 "The kings who lived sensuously with her and merchants will mourn because no one wants their cargoes."*

The harlot engaged in commerce and sorcery. She traded in the spices of the anointing oil and incense and bodies and souls of men. The blood of the slain upon the earth was in her. Rev. 18:9-21. God tells

His people to come out of her. This means it's possible for them to be in her. Rev. 18:4. She often lures his people back in since she controls the monetary systems of the earth and seduces the elect.

Think of the idol of mammon. Money is a huge lure to idolatry to take part in the harlot. Another lure is popularity or acceptance. The harlot accepts us, but at a price. The price is a close relationship with God. To His people, He says, "come out of her."

Luke 12 marks for us the seduction of the harlot. A rich man stored up goods in many barns so he could retire. He thought he was wise, but his wealth seduced him. Luke 12:20 *"But God said to him, 'You fool! This very night your soul is required of you; and now who will own what you have prepared?' 21So is the man who stores up treasure for himself and is not rich toward God."*

Again, Luke 12 *tells us not to fear about what we eat, drink or with what we are clothed. 30 "For all these things the nations of the world eagerly seek; but your Father knows that you need these things. 31 But seek His kingdom, and these things will be added to you. 32 Do not be afraid, little flock, for your Father has chosen gladly to give you the kingdom."*

Nations seek these things. The harlot seeks these things. Believers are not to seek them, but rather seek the kingdom and the righteousness of God. *"Come out of her my people."*

The harlot has always been with us. God judges her, but she is active now in the church. In some locations, she is the church. God is calling us out. Will we listen?

Her work is hard to see. Seduction obscures her activity. If we have a gap, an area of fear, she can work through this fear. The Harlot tells us we have to accept this better job. It's ok that we will seldom see our family because we show love through providing. Or she will tell us God is not providing, so we need to provide for ourselves. Or this new position is God's provision. The area of weakness is fear. The enemy loves to use our fears to keep us away from God's will which means keep us away from God. After a while, we do not notice we are not rich toward God and our heart is captured by the idolatry of fear and performance-based living. We must make our way because we did not choose to know God and to seek His kingdom. We did not believe if we seek Him, He takes care of our finances and our lives. Thus, we fell back on self-effort.

Rev. 19:1 'After these things I heard something like a loud voice of a great multitude in heaven, saying, Hallelujah! Salvation and glory and power belong to our God; 2BECAUSE HIS JUDGMENTS ARE

TRUE AND RIGHTEOUS; for He has judged the great harlot who was corrupting the earth with her immorality, and HE HAS AVENGED THE BLOOD OF HIS BOND-SERVANTS ON HER.3 And a second time they said, "Hallelujah! HER SMOKE RISES UP FOREVER AND EVER.4 And the twenty-four elders and the four living creatures fell down and worshiped God who sits on the throne saying, "Amen. Hallelujah!"5 And a voice came from the throne, saying.'

Immediately, following the harlot's judgment heaven breaks into song praising and worshipping God who judged her. For millennia heaven waited on this day. Then a voice from the throne says:

Bondservants

"Give praise to our God, all you His bondservants, you who fear Him, the small and the great."

The Lord speaks to His bondservants, His willing slaves. He judged the harlot. His bond-servants came out of her. They choose God and the fear and worship of God over the glittering enticements of the world system. Those who delight themselves in the Lord receive everything they need and God with it. These slaves of Christ can tell the difference between the real and the false. They experienced the false and received in their lives the destruction the false brings. They paid the price for their idolatry and turned to God with passion. These over-comers fought through the enticements until nothing, but Christ held them, and only Christ was Lord.

This remnant called to those captured by the harlot. Some listened, but many did not. Like the rich man of Luke 12, those who did not listen are fools, for they joined the harlot and called it God.

The backdrop of the ready bride, then, is the harlot's judgment. While the harlot's smoke rises, we see the bride. Picture the obliteration of the harlot and listen to this introduction to the bride.

Rev. 19:6"Then I heard something like the voice of a great multitude and like the sound of many waters and like the sound of mighty peals of thunder, saying, Hallelujah! For the Lord our God, the Almighty, reigns. 7 Let us rejoice and be glad and give the glory to Him, for the marriage of the Lamb has come and His bride has made herself ready. 8 It was given to her to clothe herself in fine linen, bright and clean; for the fine linen is the righteous acts of the saints."

Those remnant people sought His kingdom and His righteousness. They forsook the enticements of the harlot and trusted in Him alone. Fear causes self-effort. Instead, they exchanged fear for total trust in God. This was hard work. They had to stand for their souls and not give in to weariness. They are the Kingdom of God people.

Hear the bride give glory to God. Their voices raised sound like the voice of the Lord. Rev 1:15b, *"and His voice was like the sound of many waters."* Scripture tells us we will become like Him. This scripture shows us we will sound like him as we worship.

For Reflection
What characteristics of the Harlot do you have or cooperate with? Repent of these and commit to changing habits and patterns with the Lord's help.

Prayer
God help! I didn't know I was so influenced. Remind me when I slide toward the Harlot system. Convict me and no matter what it takes, set me free.

PART FOUR
CHAPTER 13
The Bride Comes Forth

Called to Radical Obedience and Intimacy

To understand the intimacy with and obedience to our benevolent King, we must look to John 17. This is the prayer our Bridegroom prayed to His Father before He suffered and died.

John 17:1 "Jesus spoke these things; and lifting up His eyes to heaven, He said, 'Father, the hour has come; glorify Your Son, that the Son may glorify You, 2 even as You gave Him authority over all flesh, that to all whom You have given Him, He may give eternal life. 3 This is eternal life, that they may know You, the only true God, and Jesus Christ whom You have sent. 4 I glorified You on the earth, having accomplished the work which You have given Me to do. 5 Now, Father, glorify Me together with Yourself, with the glory which I had with You before the world was.'"

In this last prayer of Jesus, He speaks of the glory that comes to the Father through His death and resurrection and the eternal life that results from these events. Then He says He glorified the Father during His earthly life by obedience to carry out the work the Father gave Him. The result of this was Jesus being glorified with the glory He had before He left the Father to live among us.

He calls us to the same obedience He practiced while He was with us. Further, He calls us to intimacy. He expects us to have conversations with Him as a bride has with her husband. Jesus practiced this intimacy with the Father when He walked among us. Though these two things may appear opposite in American culture or any democracy, they are not in the Kingdom of Heaven.

He is king. He is the King of all other Kings and deserves and must have total obedience. Our King presides over a kingdom, not a democracy. Because He is all-knowing, He knows best. The Lord does not demand obedience because He is a megalomaniac. He knows best because He is God.

He is also love. Jesus is the One who created everything we can see so He could have a bride with which to fellowship and to whom He could show His great love. If we stay connected to Him intimately, we discover that obedience brings with it more intimacy. We will understand we can trust His heart and His love, and He will only do us ultimate good.

Most of us agree with the above statements if we have attended a gospel-preaching church. But many of us do not practice obedience and trust and, so, we have little intimacy with Him.

Waiting on God

Is. 50:10-11 teaches us an important lesson:

10 "Who is among you that fears the LORD, That obeys the voice of his servant, That walks in darkness and has no light? Let him trust in the name of the LORD and rely on his God. "

11 "Behold, all you who kindle a fire, Who encircle yourselves with firebrands, Walk in the light of your fire And among the brands you have set ablaze. This you will have from My hand: You will lie down in torment."

The first point of this passage is the person who fears the Lord obeys. Then scripture tells us how obedience looks. If we walk in darkness, we are to trust in the name of the Lord and rely on Him.

The name of our King described who He was. His name included His character, function, power, purpose or a message. Jesus name means Savior and Christ means The Anointed. He is sent by the Father, and so carries the power and glory of the One who sent Him.

In that day, the banners the troops carried into battle have the name of the king emblazoned on them. If the king's name was great, other nations that were inferior seeing this would tremble in fear.

There is no higher name than God. No power can stand against Him. So, we can trust Him in every circumstance; but we struggle with this because of unbelief until we learn better.

Verse 11 tells us what we must not do. When darkness is all we can see, we are not to light our light, or we will lie down in torment. When we do not trust God, we are moving in fear and *"fear has torment"* 1 Jn. 4:18. The word torment is better translated as punishment and is present tense. So, punishment is now, ongoing and inherent in the fear. If we indulge fear, the punishment continues.

It is best-said fear is the punishment. Because we fear and do not trust, we light our fires until we learn that does not work. Lighting our fire is an attempt to ease our suffering due to, the event that brought the darkness. What happens instead is more suffering, either as ongoing or deeper suffering, because of the fear to which we yielded. Fear causes suffering.

So often we think of obedience as something that God wants us to do or a great call of God we need to fulfill. Often obedience is staying in the dark until He brings the light or remaining faithful in winter until He brings the spring. This requires trusting with all our heart. (Prov. 3:5-6) Trust is a process and develops over time as we wait on God. Our part is to choose trust while waiting in the darkness.

A friend told me a true story. On his way to a commuter train, he saw a woman with a sign that said, "Obey God." It was frigid and snowing. So, he approached her and asked, "Ma'am, why are you holding that sign out here in this weather?" She told him, "Because I did not obey God."

He got on his commuter train and was sitting there mulling over this conversation when God said to him, "Pray with these people." He jumped up and said to the people present, "Could you bow your heads while we pray." Then he prayed for those present as they bowed their heads.

The woman's experience put the fear of God in him. Can you imagine the commuter's conversation around their dinner tables that night?

Keys to Intimacy

Obedience and trust are the keys to intimacy. Jesus partook of our human condition, so He might understand what we face and become perfect through suffering *(Heb. 2)*. This is the reason He is qualified to judge us. He became human, so He could understand first-hand the things that tempt us. Then He tells us in *Heb. 3:1 NIV* that because of what He did, we are to fix our thoughts on Jesus. Fixing our thoughts is key to obedience and trust. The thought patterns are familiar to us and would keep us looking to our own devices. When we do not trust, we spend our time trying to make life work.

Today If You Hear

Hebrews gives us more insight. *Heb. 3:7 "Therefore, just as the Holy Spirit says, 'Today if you hear His voice, 8. Do not harden your hearts as when they provoked Me, As in the day of trial in the wilderness,'"*

First, we understand that today is the day we hear His voice. We often live in the past with regrets and a sense of failure. We live in fear of the future. These things keep us from hearing His voice today. We must make a conscious choice to hear His voice. If we do not, like the Israelites in the wilderness, we harden our hearts. The more we choose disobedience and lack of trust because of wounds of the past and fear of the future, the harder our hearts become.

Matt. 7:21 "Not everyone who says to Me, 'Lord, Lord,' will enter the kingdom of heaven, but he who does the will of My Father who is in heaven will enter. 22 Many will say to Me on that day, 'Lord, Lord, did we not prophesy in Your name, and in Your name cast out demons, and in Your name perform many miracles?' 23 And then I will declare to them, 'I never knew you; depart from Me, you who practice lawlessness.'"

This scripture is clear. There are some who believe they are serving God, but if they work their agenda, even if they move in the spiritual gifts listed throughout the New Testament, they practice lawlessness.

The word provoked in *Heb. 3:8* in the New American Standard Version, the NIV interprets as rebellion. When we refuse to obey and refuse to listen, so we might know what to obey, we are practicing rebellion and lawlessness.

Fear and Rebellion

The root of rebellion, disobedience, and lawlessness is fear. We rebel and disobey because we do not trust God's heart for us. Fear that His will is not our best choice stalks us. We fear Him because we do not know Him. If we knew Him, we would understand that we can trust Him to always work for our ultimate good. (For more about fear, read *Bridegroom's Song*.)

This next scripture shows what it looks like when one experiences true conversion.

1John 2:15 "Do not love the world or anything in the world. If anyone loves the world, the love of the Father is not in him.16 For everything in the world — the cravings of sinful man, the lust of his eyes and the boasting of what he has and does — comes not from the Father but from the world.17 The world and its desires pass away, but the man who does the will of God lives forever."

The person who does God's will inherits eternal life. How can this be? We could believe with our mind and change many behaviors, even entering full-time Christian work, yet do not know Christ. Our will must undergo conversion. When God converts our will, our emotions will follow. If because of fear of the future, our emotional wounds and self-interest we do not obey, we may not be His. If we choose the world's ways, rather than obedience, scripture tells us the love of the Father is not in us.

Babies are not good at obeying until trained by their parents. Even Jesus learned obedience through suffering. So, these scriptures are not referring to believers early in the process of growth. These scriptures refer to yielding to His Lordship over the whole of our life. New believers must yield their will many times until yielding becomes a way of life.

Rom. 6:11 "In the same way, count yourselves dead to sin but alive to God in Christ Jesus.12 Therefore do not let sin reign in your mortal body so that you obey its evil desires."

If we do not obey God and choose the truth that we are dead to sin, we will instead obey sin. We find one reason for this response in *John 10:10 "The thief comes only to steal and kill and destroy; I have come that they may have life and have it to the full."* The word steal means to steal by deception. Deception rules our lives before knowing Christ, and after coming to Him, we still struggle in many areas. The enemy first deceives, then he kills and destroys.

Because of this, He tells us to fix our thoughts on Jesus and consider His suffering. This helps us understand that He only wants our good. If we consider what He said and did, we learn He is trustworthy. But, if we live by the lies we believe about life, we will not make the correct choices. Notice the word choice and choices throughout this chapter. This is no accident; obedience and trust are always a choice.

Prov. 3:5 "Trust in the Lord with all your heart and lean not on your own understanding; 6 in all your ways acknowledge him, and he will make your paths straight."

The instruction to trust is a command. Again, we can opt to trust. He instructs us to trust with all our heart and scripture tells us how to do this. We are to lean not on our own understanding. To trust, we must make a conscious choice to lean on God. This means giving up our will and agenda and choosing to believe God's plan for us is best. We cannot do this without the Holy Spirit's help. But God lives within us to help us live the life to which He calls us.

So, *Hebrews 3:1* tells us to fix our thoughts on Jesus or consider and understand Him. And *Hebrews 12:2-3* tells us to fix our eyes on him.

Heb. 12:2 "Let us fix our eyes on Jesus, the author and perfecter of our faith, who for the joy set before him endured the cross, scorning its shame, and sat down at the right hand of the throne of God. 3 Consider him who endured such opposition from sinful men, so that you will not grow weary and lose heart."

Again, we must fix our eyes on Jesus. In fact, we must choose Him moment-by-moment and hour-by-hour. He will perfect our faith, but He cannot if we do not choose Him.

"for the joy set before Him, He endured the cross."

We were the joy "set before Him," and He showed us how to choose obedience, trust, and intimacy. If we set Him before us, if we see Him and fix our thoughts on Him, we will become like Him. When He died, He showed us how to live, how to die, and how to fix our focus on Him. The book of Hebrews talks of a Sabbath rest into which we are to enter. This rest is impossible apart from obedience. The concept of Sabbath rest means we cease from our works. What this means is we work the works of God. We obey. To obey, we must trust. *Hebrews 3:18-19* tells us the Israelites could not enter the rest of God in the wilderness because of disobedience. Verse 19 says they did not enter because of unbelief. Unbelief precedes disobedience.

We must choose trust and obedience despite evidence to the contrary. But we struggle. So, God gave us instruction to help us.

Heb. 4:12 "For the word of God is living and active. Sharper than any double-edged sword, it penetrates even to dividing soul and spirit, joints and marrow; it judges the thoughts and attitudes of the heart. 13 Nothing in all creation is hidden from God's sight. Everything is uncovered and laid bare before the eyes of him to whom we must give account."

*Heb. 4:14 "Therefore, since we have a great high priest who has gone through the heavens, Jesus the Son of God, let us hold firmly to the faith we **profess 15 For we do not have a high priest who is unable to sympathize with our weaknesses, but we have one who has been tempted in every way, just as we are — yet was without sin. 16 Let** us then approach the throne of grace with confidence, so that we may receive mercy and find grace to help us in our time of need."*

Along with fixing out thoughts and eyes on Jesus, we need to apply the living and active word of God to our lives. We must read and study the word. We must speak the truth against the deception illustrated in *John 10:10*. First, the enemy steals by deception, then he kills the life and truth of God, and then he destroys the lives of men. But the word of God penetrates and divides everything and shows what exists. So, we must be warriors in the word and hold firmly to the faith. We have mercy and the grace of God to help us if we receive His provision in faith.

We must stand against the lies of the enemy and not continue to give territory to him in our lives. Our choice must be for the Bridegroom, no matter how difficult the path is . He chose us. Now we must choose Him.

We have the living and active word, and our Holy God's presence living in us to help us choose truth, obedience, and intimacy with Him.

For Reflection

1. Do you have an area where you are struggling with trust? Confess this to the Lord. Then listen to what He says. Keep this problem before Him in prayer until you resolve it.

2. Listen to the Lord for any areas of disobedience in your life. Confess your sin as He shows you. Listen for what He says to you. Continue to hold this before Him in prayer until resolved.

Prayer

Lord, help me quit lighting my fire and wait upon You in the darkness. Empower me to trust with my whole heart, trust Your word and apply it to my life. I fix my eyes on You. Help me continue to do so.

CHAPTER 14
Intimacy Requires Hearing

Listening

Obedience requires hearing the voice of God, and hearing intimately connects us to God. We cannot obey if we cannot hear and we cannot hear if we do not take time to listen. For instance, if we marry someone and then never listen to the heart of our spouse, we will not have a successful marriage.

Song 1:4 gives us another look at the first blush of knowing Him.

"Take me away with you—let us hurry! Let the king bring me into his chambers."

In this passage, chambers mean His innermost apartment. The bride is crying out for Him to draw her into intimacy with Him. In the timeline of the Song, she has just met Him. She awaits the betrothal and the consummation of the marriage. But she is thinking ahead, wanting to experience the closeness that comes because of marriage. This yearning is a part of the new believer's experience and is to be a part of our lives over the years, as the next passage of scripture shows us.

Psa. 27:4 "One thing I have asked from the Lord, that I shall seek: That I may dwell in the house of the Lord all the days of my life, To behold the beauty of the Lord, and to meditate in His temple. "

Notice this says all the days of my life. This verse highlights meditating in His temple. This includes hearing His voice.

Revelation 21 shows us his city with the Lamb as our lamp. Forever we will behold His beauty and meditate on His glory, grace, love, and his other attributes. Further, we are to want this now.

Winter's End

He displays his heart's desire for fellowship with us in *Song 2:10"My beloved responded and said to me, 'Arise, my darling, my beautiful one, And come along. 11 For behold, the winter is past, The rain is over and gone. 12 The flowers have already appeared in the land; The time has arrived for pruning the vines, And the voice of the turtledove has been heard in our land. 13 The fig tree has ripened its figs, And the vines in blossom have given forth their fragrance. Arise, my darling, my beautiful one, And come along!'"*

God speaks this to the bride after she has endured a long winter season; winter was so long, and she finds herself reluctant to respond. Winter caused her to question all she guided her life by, and it wounded her so deeply that hope is missing from her life.

Without winter, spring has no meaning and no extra joy. Indeed, the promise of spring after the dreariness of winter brings renewed hope. What appears dead sprouts with the life we forgot was possible. This discourse by the Bridegroom is the first hint that spring may be possible

Winter Season
Winter, dead, barren, cold,
stretching on it seems forever.
No fruitfulness, no life, and nothing to give hope.
Joy lies frozen under the snow.
It looks like never again will life flourish.
All is gone.

But then the crocus blooms
through the cold.
That which appeared forever was transient.
The barrenness ends with the melting.
And joy blooms again.

Many experienced winter that is so deep; the concept of spring has become foreign. Clearly, years of winter without a spring, make it impossible to think of change. It is in this dark season that the Lord comes to us to say spring is here. We can choose. We can stay where we are, so we do not risk more pain, or we can trust Him and go with Him. He does not tell us where He is taking us, only that He invites us to come with Him. He yearns to journey with us. Then He invites us into His presence.

Song 2:14 "O my dove, in the clefts of the rock,

In the secret place of the steep pathway,

Let me see your form, Let me hear your voice;

For your voice is sweet, And your form is lovely."

He calls us into the secret place of His presence. It is along a steep pathway, but we have known little else. Rather, the mountains of difficulty have been our life. Will we climb again?

That which helps us choose Him is the rest of His words to us. He wants to see our form and hear our voice. He calls our voice sweet, and we are lovely to Him. During long years of winter with no spring, one thing remains true for His bride. She loves Him and longs to be with Him. No matter how deep the pain and how unhealed the wounds which He allowed, she wants Him.

If you are being called out of that winter season listen to His invitation. *"Let me see you, let me hear your voice, for your voice is sweet, and you are lovely."* Winter has told you otherwise, but His appeal is the truth. Will you choose the truth He speaks to you or the lie of winter?

Song 4:8 "Come with me from Lebanon, my bride, 9 You have stolen my heart, my sister, my bride; you have stolen my heart with one glance of your eyes, with one jewel of your necklace."

Repeatedly, throughout Song of Songs, He cries out with a yearning for us. He invites us to go with Him. He describes the way He sees us.

There are four in-depth portrayals of us in Song of Songs. (For more on this subject, read *Bridegroom's Song*.) These descriptions show us what He saw when He went to Calvary for us. *"who for the joy set before him endured the cross, scorning its shame" (Heb. 12:2)*. We were the joy set before Him. Song of Songs describes what He saw as He walked the way to Calvary and death. He fixed His eyes on us so that He could die for us.

The truth is, He created the world so He could have a bride, so He could have you. This God of All gods yearns for fellowship with you. This King wants you. To be sure, He yearns for you now and wants you to be ready to spend eternity with Him in fellowship so sweet, no language can describe it.

The book of Genesis begins with intimacy with man in the garden. The book of Revelation ends with intimacy with the bride as the New Jerusalem.

History is the Story of His desire for Intimacy with Us.

Gen. 3:8 "And they heard the voice of the Lord God walking in the garden in the cool of the day:" The Lord communed with Adam and Eve by His voice. In the garden, they had what we long for, God speaking to them regularly. Man lost this through sin, but Christ's death restored it if we will have it.

In *Ex. 19* He told the Israelites if they obeyed his voice, he would make them His own possession or treasure, a kingdom of priests and a holy nation. Because of fear, they did not consent to Him leading by His voice. *Ex.19 and Jere. 7:22-25.* Being led by His voice means intimacy and requires obedience.

Obedience without intimacy is law. Intimacy is not possible without obedience, for disobedience breaks the covenant and stops the voice of God. So, Christ died to set up the covenant by His voice with all who respond to the invitation to intimacy and obedience.

Then, in *Revelation 21*, we see the bride as a city with the Lord himself the light of that place. His glory is the illumination of the bride. Her heart has sought the light of that glory, the light of that blessed face for the whole of her Christian experience. She came to understand while here on earth that obedience's glorious reward is intimacy with Christ. There is no better reward in life or eternity, and no price of obedience too high to eclipse intimacy's glory.

Do not allow the enemy's strategies to steal this great love. There is none greater. In reality, his love belongs to you. This requires trust, so you choose obedience.

Trust has the word of God woven into the tapestry of our lives, replacing the threads of lies woven by the enemy. Violence is a prerequisite for this. We must seize His truth as if only this could save our lives, because only His truth will.

Choosing this love and our Lover again and again over every surrounding enticement must become our life. We must give up control and surrender as a bride to her bridegroom on her wedding night. All she knows is that the one who paid her bridal price with His blood loves her and she is his..

For Reflection

1. Confess to the Lord your wrong attitudes toward intimacy. Tell Him what you will change.

2. What have you discovered in this chapter that helps you understand His red-hot love? Journal this and read it over these next few weeks until your ideas about His love change permanently.

Prayer

The longer I know you, Lord, the more I realize I cannot think correctly unless You redeem every thought and motivation of my heart. Help me do your will. and want You above everything and to stop my wrongheaded ways of thinking. I want to seek You more than the air I breathe.

CHAPTER 15

Put on Your Wedding Garment

How Do We Get Our Wedding Garment

Scripture tells us we are to put on Jesus Christ, put on our wedding garment, and put on faith and love (1Thess. 5:8), plus our new self (Eph. 4:20-28) and our armor (Eph. 6). Further, we must put off our old self. His bride must understand what we put off and on. Ultimately, we are to put on a bridal garment. But what is our bridal garment and how do we get it? For, a general understanding of wedding garments this parable of Jesus gives us a first look:

Matt. 22:1 "'Jesus spoke to them again in parables, saying, 2The kingdom of heaven may be compared to a king who gave a wedding feast for his son. 3 And he sent out his slaves to call those who had been invited to the wedding feast, and they were unwilling to come. 4 Again he sent out other slaves saying, 'Tell those who have been invited, "Behold, I have prepared my dinner; my oxen and my fattened livestock are all butchered and everything is ready; come to the wedding feast.' 5 But they paid no attention and went their way, one to his own farm, another to his business, 6 and the rest seized his slaves and mistreated them and killed them.'"

This passage states that the king invited people to a wedding feast, but they chose not to come. Besides, this passage shows us four ways we refuse to get ready for the wedding feast.

To get ready, they would have to put off their plans and accept the king's plan or exchange their will and plans for his will and plans. So, one lesson in this scripture is a readiness to do the king's will.

Types of "Believers"

These people unwilling to attend are the unsaved that hear the message and decide against it, or those who agree intellectually with this message that Jesus is Savior and Lord, but do not embrace Lordship and heart belief.

In today's church, many believe this way. Further, we have so watered the gospel we tell people if they believe Jesus is Savior, He will make life easier. We don't tell them it will cost them everything and they will need to make Him Lord of their life. Many today attend our churches and think they are "saved," but without life change, because there was no true conversion.

There are many cultural Christians. They have grown up in the church and know doctrine. These worship, sing in the choir, attend Bible study, but they do not know Him as Lord and Savior. They embrace Christian culture, but they have not embraced Him.

The second group in this parable paid no attention because they were too busy making a living or serving. One went off to his field, another to his business. This could mean busy with church work. When "church" becomes the focus rather than intimately knowing the Lord, we miss His invitation while thinking we are serving Him. We tell ourselves we are following Him while we are serving our egos or our scarred sense of self.

With self deeply wounded, we often develop behaviors of service to others that help us feel better but keep us from the Lord himself. These behaviors can find their expression in Christian service.

We may do Christian service to receive praise from others or hold off feeling worthless; in doing that, we are not walking in His life. Others want the praise of men because they believe they deserve it. In addition, many in this category quote scriptures about salvation being only by grace, but they serve to win points with God or people. Others serve God to prove to themselves so they perform well enough for love and acceptance.

Those who paid no attention were saying the wedding banquet is not important enough to even notice. The king's heart yearning was not their focus. Instead, one returned to his farm, another to his business. They were busy with other things because they do not know the king's heart.

Mark 4:18 "And others are the ones on whom seed was sown among the thorns; these are the ones who have heard the word, 19 but the worries of the world, and the deceitfulness of riches, and the desires for other things enter in and choke the word, and it becomes unfruitful."

This group has unfruitful soil. They have not allowed the Lord to help remove the thorns in their soil. They hang on to that which makes them idolaters. Many say they worship God, but they worship their accomplishments. They get their sense of worth from their performance rather than from the One who gave himself for them.

Not only are their riches deceitful, so is their heart. They have not made Jesus Lord and His cross central. Further, they did not allow Him to transplant His heart within them in exchange for their hard heart. In truth, humans hang on to vanity and call it the truth. They involve themselves in the world's system characterized by the harlot, but are unaware. The watered-down under-standing of the role of the cross in today's church culture keeps them from seeing the truth. Unlike the bride who forsakes the world, those who pay no attention to the King, seek the world's enticements.

Many true believers likely did the same for a season and then have seen their performance-based orientation and their idolatrous lifestyle and repented. They put off the world's ways and submitted to God, putting on Christ. Their soil is free of thorns.

The next type of person who did not go to the wedding banquet persecuted those who carried the message. In the end, they killed the king's servants. Likely, they did this because they disliked the message or felt it "too much." That means too much commitment, time, or too much of their divided heart expected. Thus, they did not want to hear the message to attend the wedding banquet because it required something from them.

The Bridal Message

This message is what Jesus came to earth to deliver. He is the Bridegroom. The bridal price was His life. Most of the religious leaders of the day missed Him. For the Pharisees, He claims to be God, His cry against their hypocrisy and religious duplicity were "too much." In truth, the Pharisees blamed and shamed Him, put Him on public display, then killed Him. Then, they said it was His fault. The same happens to many servants of the King today.

Another cause of persecution is envy. Scripture tells us Jesus died because the Pharisees envied Him. He was a threat to their power over the people. *(Mk. 15:10, Ja.3: 14-16).*

Persecution

Those who do not affirm the call to the wedding banquet for the Son may, like the Pharisees, persecute those who call them to the banquet. This has taken place throughout the ages. Likewise, it takes place now. Persecution comes to those who cry out to woo the church to know Him as Bridegroom. The Pharisee's attitude that led to the death of the Bridegroom is still active. In reality, it happens because it's the persecuted person's fault. Society tells the persecuted they are the problem and their message is "too much".

Those who persecuted the messengers the king sent believed the message to attend the wedding banquet was antithetical to their truth or that their truth was more important. Many do not believe getting ready for the wedding banquet is crucial if we get our doctrine "right." Right doctrine is an essential step in Christian life, but we can twist the truth and make it into error. In like fashion, we can call our ideas doctrine and teach them to others. This is knowledge, but not truth. Doctrine is one facet of a precious stone. An intimate relationship is another facet. Sadly, if we have knowledge without a relationship, we can become prideful about our knowledge and stuck there.

When close, we hear His voice, and He explains the scriptures to us. His Spirit helps us realize what the word means. To put it another way, if we try to understand without the Spirit, we end up with church splits and denominations. Church history is littered with efforts to find belief apart from the Spirit of God.

The scripture below shows the underlying belief of the "church" of Jesus' day.

Mark 7:6 "Rightly did Isaiah prophesy of you hypocrites, as it is written: 'THIS PEOPLE HONORS ME WITH THEIR LIPS, BUT THEIR HEART IS FAR AWAY FROM ME.7 'BUT IN VAIN DO THEY WORSHIP ME, TEACHING AS DOCTRINES THE PRECEPTS OF MEN.' 8 Neglecting the commandment of God, you hold to the tradition of men."

The Pharisees convinced themselves that their doctrine was correct, but they missed the Bridegroom. They worshipped in vain. They studied much, but they did not study to know God. Instead, their study was to impress men (*Matt. 23*).

Man's doctrines lead us to kill the messengers the King sends to invite us to the wedding banquet. The Pharisees did this when the Bridegroom himself invited them. If we don't kill them, we can reject them, exclude them, shame them and tell them the persecution is their fault.

It is important that we allow the Lord to cleanse our hearts of our improper motives, so we are ready for the wedding, and put on our wedding garment. For this, we need to look past earth's rewards and keep our focus on the Lord, our heavenly reward.

For Reflection

1. Ask the Lord to show you if you are refusing the message to get ready for the wedding. Write whatever He shows you and pray until He tells you your heart is in alignment with His.

2. Are you a cultural Christian or is Jesus Lord of all? Do you live for your plans or Him? Commit to Him today to make Him Lord of every aspect of your life.

3. If you harmed His messengers, talk to God about this and make it right with Him and with those you harmed.

Prayer

Bridegroom Lamb, grant me forgiveness for treating the desire of Your heart so lightly. Draw me ever nearer, so I respond with total love to You. Draw me, Lord. Help me be willing to say yes to each step on this journey. I permit You to drag me there if You must. Do not leave me in my present condition but draw me on into the center of Your will. May Your will become more important than my next breath?

CHAPTER 16
Putting Off the Old and
Putting on the New

The Fourth Refusal

There is a fourth way the king's subjects refused the king.

Matt. 22:11 "But when the king came in to look over the dinner guests, he saw a man there who was not dressed in wedding clothes, 12 and he said to him, 'Friend, how did you come in here without wedding clothes?' And the man was speechless. 13 Then the king said to the servants, 'Bind him hand and foot, and throw him into the outer darkness; in that place there will be weeping and gnashing of teeth.' 14 For many are called, but few are chosen.'"

The king invited these guests to the wedding banquet after the first group refused. The custom was for the king to give wedding clothes to wedding guests sponsored by him on that day. This is also true of the bride, according to *Revelation 19:7-8*. However, the man in this story chose not to wear the clothes the King provided. He thought the clothes he owned were suitable. So, what are the King's expectations?

The Pharisees and Us

This parable sets between two diatribes by Jesus against the Pharisees. So, we could assume that the Lord's message in these other two parables relates to the answer. He addresses the Pharisees' hypocrisy in the two parables that bookend this passage. Hypocrisy is the Greek word for an actor. Hypocrisy, play-acting and our rationalization and denial keep us from seeing the lies within our lives. Unbelievably, we choose hypocrisy even unconsciously. We do this to stop future hurt. We devise a false identity we think will keep people from seeing the "truth," the horrible shame that got us hurt.

This false identity covers up the "real" identity we have. Real is in quotes because the real identity is not real either, but we believe it of ourselves, and we feel shame because of it. Others put this identity on us by their actions or the enemy's tactics and lies. Sadly, even though it's a lie, it has become ours, and we own it and protect it as if it were precious.

This wounding happens while we are young. Because we are young, we think no one must know, so we devise this more pleasing identity. We put on a mask announcing this new identity to anyone we meet. No one can know our "truth." Isaiah spoke of this problem thousands of years ago.

IS. 28:15C "For we have made falsehood our refuge and we have concealed ourselves with deception."

Or to say it another way we made lies our refuge and have hidden with those lies. The Lord must become our refuge, not the lies we accept about ourselves.

At odds with these two false identities, is our real identity as believers. We are in Christ. We are His, chosen, set apart and dearly loved. But often we only pay these truths lip service because we are so busy playing the role that goes with our mask or masks. Instead, we are busy covering up what we regard as the "real" us, but it's not real. It is a lie perpetrated by the enemy and meant to shame us, bind us and drive us to hypocrisy. The enemy loves hypocrisy. He loves acting. He acts because he lies constantly.

We present this self to others instead of embracing the truth. The work of God is to set us free from the false identity that deludes us and keeps us from him. This takes years and multiple hours in his word and presence. We cannot put on our wedding garment when this clothes us first. We believe we are clothed and need nothing. *(Rev. 3:17)*. So, we refuse the wedding garment.

What Mask Do You Wear

In brief, in the Greek theater of Bible times, the hypocrite (actor) has several masks in their hand. They put up a different mask for each part they played. Undeniably, this presents a picture of what we do to survive emotionally when we experience brokenness without healing.

The man without wedding clothes was saying, "What I am wearing (which announces who I believe I am) is good enough. I don't need what the King gives." These are the sins of pride and self-sufficiency. They are two things that commonly go with false identities. He was saying, "I am rich and need nothing." *(Rev. 3:17)* He needed to put off what he was wearing to put on what the King provided.

This man made a conscious choice not to wear clothes the King provided. Unless we submit to the difficulty that sets us free, we do this too. We do not realize we are wearing a deceptive identity. We must put off what we believe about ourselves to receive the truth. Our deception is so deep, we cannot see the truth unless we live a life of total commitment. Only as we commit and recommit to knowing God will He be able to bring freedom to us. Indeed, in His presence and through suffering, He can show us our false self (idol). Because suffering is a part of this retraining, a belief system without carrying our cross daily can keep us from the healing we need.

Have you ever known someone amid a conflict with other friends or family? They keep on telling you who they are and stating, "I am not that kind of person." But you notice they are the instigator or at least part of the problem. You saw a false identity. The scripture states that the heart of man is wicked and beyond our knowing *(Jer. 17:6)*. We often think we know ourselves when we do not. This is because deception blinds us to the truth. The Lord knows our hearts, however (Rev. 2:23). This false identity does not announce itself well. Since false identities hide under protective layers, we have trouble seeing through them. We portray what we believe in subtle ways. We seldom know why we do the things we do.

Awake

Rom. 13:11 "Do this, knowing the time, that it is already the hour for you to awaken from sleep; for now, salvation is nearer to us than when we believed. 12 The night is almost gone, and the day is near. Therefore, let us lay aside the deeds of darkness and put on the armor of light.13 Let us behave properly as in the day, not in carousing and drunkenness, not in sexual promiscuity and sensuality, not in strife and jealousy.14 But put on the Lord Jesus Christ and make no provision for the flesh in regard to its lusts."

The passage above has an urgency to awaken from sleep and get dressed. We are to put on armor and the Lord Jesus Christ. Before either of these can take place, we must lay aside the deeds of darkness. To put on the day's clothing, we must take off whatever we wore to sleep. Also, we wear armor over something, or it rubs our skin raw. So, we put off darkness and put on Christ and His righteousness.

Laying aside the deeds of darkness includes not carousing. Carousing was often a loud party that paraded through the streets, giving honor to another god with sexual debauchery. [xxvi] Sex was worship to these other gods. It still is today. We worship our gods of sexual license in many nations.

We are to put off drunkenness, sexual promiscuity, sensuality, strife, and jealousy. These things can keep us from putting on our armor, our wedding garment, and the Lord Jesus Christ.

Think of this. Carousing included honor to other gods. In fact, these gods were so much a part of the culture they did not recognize them as wrong. Idolatry could be the reason the King's subjects were not ready. Service to many gods distracts us too much to see the urgency to get ready. In wealthy nations, some of those gods are comfort, convenience, mammon, leisure, entertainment, selfishness, etc.

In *Matthew 22* the gods served could have been the gods who promised abundant crops or business success. Certainly, those who did not come to the banquet felt that serving their agenda, their idol god, was more important than serving the king. The *Matthew 22* passage starts with the statement *"the kingdom of heaven is like."* Thus, the Lord was saying this is the practice of those who claim to be His church.

Every Evil Work

In *Rom. 13* the root words that make up the word strife literally means to have "conquest over a friend"-[xxvii]. Often, we do not recognize this as keeping us from putting on our armor, our wedding garment, and the Lord Himself. Instead, we believe we are justified in our disputes. Because of this, when you see strife and jealousy together, it makes sense to look at the book of James to uncover what the Lord is saying.

James 3:13 "Who among you is wise and understanding? Let him show by his good behavior his deeds in the gentleness of wisdom. 14 But if you have bitter jealousy and selfish ambition in your heart, do not be arrogant and so lie against the truth. 15 This wisdom is not that which comes down from above, but is earthly, natural, demonic. 16 For where jealousy and selfish ambition exist, there is disorder and every evil thing,".

NIV renders the words bitter jealousy as bitter envy. The reason is that the word bitter describes this emotion. Envy and jealousy have different meanings. Envy is jealousy together with bitterness and selfish ambition. Though envy and jealousy have a shared meaning in wanting something someone else has, envy takes it several steps further. The one who envies must dispossess the person envied. Even if the envious cannot have what the envied person has, they must wrestle the coveted object from the one envied. Often, this object is the person's good standing in a congregation or group.

They want to control the person and their gifts. An example is Jezebel. She dispossessed Naboth of his vineyard by having him killed. She dispossessed the true prophets of their position by killing them. Then she controlled the Baal prophets (they ate at her table) thereby controlling the prophetic. Today, the envious still work to control God's voice to his people.

Selfish ambition is a perverted form of self-love and causes this. A synonym for selfish ambition is strife. Some translations translate the words selfish ambition as strife. Wherever this arises, strife and every evil work arise.

The envious are *"arrogant and lie against the truth."* Why would they do this? They cannot admit the problem is in their heart and choose blindness to their sin. They choose their sin rather than to put on the Lord Jesus Christ. If they were to see their problem, their idol, they must suffer to see it. That is true of our false beliefs.

Suffering is the road to freedom — those that envy cause others to suffer and insulate themselves from suffering and discovery by believing a lie. Jesus learned obedience from suffering, but many will not allow this suffering in their lives.

This "wisdom" is earthly. This means of the earth, of earthly wisdom and the earthly sphere, or of the world's system, the harlot system. It is natural, which means unspiritual.

This wisdom is demonic. This means that on one hand, this problem is unspiritual or natural. Also, the wisdom is spiritual, but the wrong spirit. Involved in this problem is demonic activity. Demons are just manifestations of the gods we serve. Or you could say the gods we serve have demons behind them. Both statements are valid.

We are idolaters at heart until God intervenes. We worship getting our way. Demons influence our thoughts to help us do this. But as believers, we must learn to put off these behaviors and not listen to the enemy's whispers.

God's Wisdom

James 3:17 "But the wisdom from above is first pure, then peaceable, gentle, reasonable, full of mercy and good fruits, unwavering, without hypocrisy. 18 And the seed whose fruit is righteousness is sown in peace by those who make peace." NASB.

True wisdom is without hypocrisy, without masks. To the extent, a person is transparent, they are approachable. Only the person who has laid aside the false identities and behavioral protections is a safe person. Only when we put these off can we truly put on the Lord Jesus Christ.

Eph. 4:20 "You, however, did not come to know Christ that way.21 Surely you heard of him and were taught in him in accordance with the truth that is in Jesus.2 You were taught, with regard to your former way of life, to put off your old self, which is being corrupted by its deceitful desires; 23 to be made new in the attitude of your minds; 24 and to put on the new self, created to be like God in true righteousness and holiness."

First, we are told to put off our old self and falsehood. Second, we put on the new self, *"created to be like God in true righteousness and holiness."* We have at our disposal the indwelling presence of God to help us receive the transformation He purchased for us. We are to become more like God as His Spirit works within us, transforming us. For this to happen, we must commit to His will rather than our agenda, (business and field). We must commit to knowing Him. Knowledge of Him must become the over-riding passion of our life.

We need to seek Him in the word and speak the truth of His word against the lies that guide our lives. If we will allow knowledge of Him to be our only passion and seek Him in His word, we will put off those things that keep us from putting on our wedding garment.

Col. 3:6 "For it is because of these things that the wrath of God will come upon the sons of disobedience, 7 and in them you also once walked, when you were living in them.8 But now you also, put them all aside: anger, wrath, malice, slander, and abusive speech from your mouth.9 Do not lie to one another, since you laid aside the old self with its evil practices, 10 and have put on the new self who is being renewed to a true knowledge according to the image of the One who created him —11 renewal in which there is no distinction between Greek and Jew, circumcised and uncircumcised, barbarian, Scythian, slave and freeman, but Christ is all, and in all. "(Emphasis mine) Christ is ALL, and He is in us helping us.

*Col. 3:12 "So, as those who have been chosen of God, holy and beloved, **put on a heart of compassion, kindness, humility, gentleness and patience;"***

In Col. 3 we see we are to "put off the old self" and to put on the new self and a "heart of compassion, kindness, humility, gentleness, and patience." We are to put on the new self in the Creator's image and put on the saint's righteous acts. So, putting off readies us to put on the new self and the righteous acts *(Rev. 19:8)* that make up the wedding garment. If we put off the old without putting on the new self, our efforts fail. We must replace the lies with the truth to support freedom from the lies.

We risk this and the suffering that goes with giving up everything we hold dear because we are beloved by Him. Indeed, in His eyes through His blood, we are perfect. *Song 4:7 "You are all beautiful my darling and there is no flaw in you."* The Lord of All lives in us to empower us for the obedience He requires of us. He sees us as "all beautiful" and without a flaw, and He is Lord.

For Reflection

1. What should you put off for your freedom? In what way does God want you to accomplish this?

2. What should you put on to replace the lies? Write how you will do this.

3. What will you change so you come to know Christ intimately?

4. Will you commit to whatever it takes to get ready for the Bridegroom? Tell Him your commitment and ask for His help. Then listen and write what He says to you.

Prayer

Lord, there is much that needs removed. I know if You pulled back the veil I would see more. Help! Show me how to align my heart with Yours. Help me put off the old self, the enemy's lies, and put on You.

Help me draw near to You and be willing for the suffering it takes to see the lies that guide my life. Since they are my identity, I know this will be painful, but You are with me. Help me not pull back from the process and most important not pull back from You. You are my hope, my help, and my only answer.

CHAPTER 17
The Wedding Rehearsal

Rehearse the Correct Things

*Heb. 12:1 "Therefore, since we have so great a cloud of witnesses surrounding us, let us also **lay aside every encumbrance and the sin which so easily entangles us, and let us run with endurance the race that is set before us, 2 fixing our eyes on Jesus, the author and perfecter of faith, who for the joy set before Him endured the cross, despising the shame, and has sat down at the right hand of the throne of God."***

Scripture encourages us to lay aside every encumbrance and focus on Jesus. This means quit rehearsing the lies that keep you from seeing who He is. Rehearse what the word says about Him and His love for you. Rehearse the truth every time the lie surfaces. This is difficult because we seldom recognize the lies. However, if we focus on Him, if we choose Him again and again, in time we will recognize those lies for what they are. We will see Him with more clarity. The same areas where before sin defeated us will yield to victory if we speak the word of God against every lie. Listening to His voice in the secret place of His presence is mandatory, so we may hear His love talk to us.

If we are to be ready, we must not only consider Him who suffered, but we too will suffer. Scripture tells us we can *"fellowship by sharing in His sufferings," Phil. 3:7-11*. We have to deny ourselves and take up our cross and follow him. *(Lu. 9:23)*.

If we even want to save our life, we will lose it *(Lu. 9:24)*. As we saw the desire to live life on our terms will cause us to lose the life He has for us. So, in complying with a focus on Jesus, we will suffer. We cannot come to Him on His terms without this being fulfilled in us. It takes our cross to wrestle from us our desires for life our way, our fight against denying ourselves and our hatred for suffering.

It is critical we yield our whole life to Him, but when we start, we do not know what this means. He shows this to us. We often think we deny ourselves, only to find out we have more to deny. When pain comes, we need to lean into it. Suffering presents the opportunity to fellowship with Him intimately. Intimate fellowship produces His likeness in us.

For centuries, the Israelites served God and mixed the reverence of other gods with their worship. This brought in child sacrifice and injustice of many sorts. Included were licentious sexual practices, since many of these other religions sanctioned temple prostitutes as a part of worship. God was calling His people to fidelity to Him alone, but they kept turning aside to other gods who allowed them to practice sin.

One day, when the bloodguilt of child sacrifice became too much, He allowed Babylon to invade and take the people of Israel not killed in the battle captive to Babylon. This happens to us as well.

Babylon and Us

When we don't understand surrender and fidelity, He warns us. If we do not listen to the warning, we end up in Babylon metaphorically through difficult circumstances. (For the story of the Babylonian captivity refers to *2 Ki. 24-25, 2 Chr. 9-36, Lamentations, Jeremiah 20-46, Ezra and Nehemiah.*)

When we dwell in Babylon, we experience confusion. Like the Israelites who lost their land, temple, livelihood, and family members, we lose everything we believed in and the things that sustained us. Often, we find ourselves bitter and angry with God. We do not realize we are in a place critical to our growth. Babylon is where God separates the true worshippers from the pretenders. Those who choose God while in Babylon are the true worshippers. Those who mix the gods of Babylon with the worship of Jehovah are impostors.

Ponder what this next scripture says about suffering.

Romans 8:18 "For I consider that the sufferings of this present time are not worthy to be compared with the glory that is to be revealed to us.19 For the anxious longing of the creation waits eagerly for the revealing of the sons of God.20 For the creation was subjected to futility, not willingly, but because of Him who subjected it, in hope 21 that the creation itself also will be set free from its slavery to corruption into the freedom of the glory of the children of God."

The Israelites had to quit reverencing other gods. Indeed, they needed to see the futile behaviors that kept them from the worship of God alone. Their agony in Babylon brings forth obedience and, therefore, the glory of God.

Our suffering sets us free from the things that keep us from reflecting His glory if we allow it. God subjected the creation to futility (Babylon) because of God's hope to free us from slavery to our futility gods to become at last His children completely surrendered.

So, suffering at the very deepest level possible is part of the training and preparation for the marriage. His sufferings and the fellowship in those sufferings is the crucial element of our wedding rehearsal. We do not agonize alone if we allow Him close during these times. As we suffer, we can have an intimate fellowship with Him.

This next passage speaks of a time of restoration after great desolation. Captive in Babylon for 70 years because of their idolatry and spiritual adultery; God released the Israelites to go back to Israel. Isaiah prophesied their defeat by Babylon 80 years before their captivity. Isaiah perceived what was coming and prophesied Judah's destruction. Jeremiah prophesied and saw the devastation with his own eyes. Babylon took the Promised Land away from the people of God's promise. Those who still sought YHWH knew they had no one to blame but themselves. During this time in Babylon, they received another promise.

Is. 49:15 "Can a woman forget her nursing child and have no compassion on the son of her womb? Even these may forget, but I will not forget you. 16 Behold, I have inscribed you on the palms of My hands; Your walls are continually before Me. 17 Your builders hurry; Your destroyers and devastators will depart from you. 18 Lift up your eyes and look around; All of them gather together, they come to you. As I live," declares the LORD, "You will surely put on all of them as jewels and bind them on as a bride. 19 For your waste and desolate places and your destroyed land — Surely now you will be too cramped for the inhabitants. And those who swallowed you will be far away.' 20 The children of whom you were bereaved will yet say in your ears, 'The place is too cramped for me; Make room for me that I may live here.' 21 "Then you will say in your heart, 'who has begotten these for me, Since I have been bereaved of my children and am barren, an exile and a wanderer? And who has reared these? Behold, I was left alone; from where did these come?'"

Those who longed for God while a captive in Babylon were familiar with this scripture when released to return to Israel, they went as a bride with great joy. They waited on this day with anticipation.

Staying in Babylon

Many more stayed in Babylon because, like the people invited to the King's wedding banquet, they did not long for what the King longed for (Matt:22) or for the land he had given them. They fixed their eyes on other things. Babylon's gods had become theirs. We can accept these other gods and worship them along with God Almighty.

The Lord told those who left Babylon to re-inhabit Israel that their destroyers will leave, and the builders come. They were to put on the builders as the jewels a bride puts on for her wedding. The people of Judah were captive 70 years. They had many wounds and thus needed healing because of sin's punishment. But if they accept the call of God to return from Babylon, restoration as a bride was theirs. He was calling them to a relationship rather than knowledge. We, too, need healing and restoration as a bride. We must have intimacy to transform us.

Babylon is necessary, so we surrender the futile ways of life passed down from our forefathers. Then we must embrace the new life given by the Bridegroom Lamb. We can only know this life as we spend time with Him in His presence and word. Similar to the Israelites before us, we worship other gods. God, in His mercy, warns us through others and His word. When we don't listen, we end up in Babylon. The word Babylon means confusion. When we come into dark months and years and cannot find our way often, we are captive. This could be a prolonged winter season characterized by loss of hope.

When we experience a Babylon time to prove our devotion, will we assimilate into this new location or learn to long for the one true God? Will Jesus become the focus?

Our promise if we come out of exile is bridal intimacy and spiritual children. These are the promises that relate to the two greatest commandments to love God with all our being and love our neighbors. Bridal intimacy brings us into total love for God. Without Babylon, we may never be free enough to experience this.

For Reflection

1. Are you in a confusing time? Do you feel as if you are in Babylon? Pray for the Lord to help you understand where he is in this for you.

2. Will you allow Him to be your comfort during this time? Will you fellowship with Him around the sufferings of Christ?

3. Let Him show you what caused your exile.

4. Continue to pray over the weeks, months and years, so He reveals other things that keep you from true intimacy.

Prayer

Lord, forgive me for the things I reverence along with You, but I cannot yet see. I want to worship only You. Set me free from the futility of my idolatry. Draw me into intimacy. You are my overriding hope.

CHAPTER 18
CITY OF WARRIORS-MORE REHEARSAL

From Futility to Warrior

Those who walk in intimacy find many challenges in their lives and many obstacles to overcome. The scripture is clear in *Romans 8*. God subjects us to futility, so He will set us free from our tendency toward sin into the freedom of the children of God. This means we will fight many spiritual battles. Some of these battles are futile; we sense that nothing we try works. This is because we trust in other gods, other behaviors not compatible with our life in God.

The book that carries more information than any other about the many positive attributes we possess in God's sight is Song of Songs. In this book, we read:

Song 4:4 "Your neck is like the tower of David, built with elegance; on it hang a thousand shields, all of them shields of warriors."

The tower of David is a watchtower with shields of war hanging on it. These shields are small shields each soldier used in close combat. This has several applications. The first application is that she is a watchtower watching for the enemy's approach. She sees the enemy coming and warns others. The second application is that the ornaments she is wearing on her neck are shields with which to engage in hand-to-hand combat. She has many shields. These are shields for her students, so they learn warfare.

One is the shield of faith in the book of Ephesians. The Lord sees her calling to warfare and knows her faith will sustain her in her calling. There are battles to win for our King of Love. She does not understand the fullness of this yet, but He sees it as He looks at her. This is the Lord's first mention of her as a warrior. Others follow.

Delightsome City With Flags Flying

Song 6:4 "You are beautiful, my darling, as Tirzah, lovely as Jerusalem, majestic as troops with banners."

The word Tirzah means delightsome. Tirzah was a city in the northern kingdom of Israel. This city was so beautiful its name was delightsome. Tirzah set on a hill. Cities set on hills have an advantage in times of warfare.

Matthew 5:14 "You are the light of the world. A city on a hill cannot be hidden.

Not only is she a city with a warfare advantage, Matthew tells us she is a light. When she wins battles for the King, the light that comes from her city draws others to her so they can discover the secret of her power and her light. Because of her power and light, the following takes place.

"The Friends say": Song 6:10'" Who is this that grows like the dawn, As beautiful as the full moon, As pure as the sun, As awesome as an army with banners?"

This bride has dawning, gradual light as others view her beauty like the moonlight at its fullest. Her purity shines with the brightest light. Sunlight sustains that which it affects. And she is an awesome army volunteer. So impressive that she resembles an entire army because she is. She has mentored others, and they have joined her in the King's battles.

The banner of the King puts fear into the hearts of the adversary. Those around the bride see her power and her light. The light of the sun generates power and causes nature's power to produce the things we need to live. However, the power seen in the Lord's bride is so vast it resembles a bannered army. It is one thing to have the Lord recognize her power by describing her as an army with banners, and another thing for others to witness it too. This means they understand the source of her power.

She is an army. She knows how to engage in warfare and how to yield to the King's power. He gives His power to her to wield on His behalf until He comes again to make every kingdom His. Further, she is to occupy until then. This means win territory and keep it. Don't yield it to the enemy. She has power for this because of His power at work within her.

Military Discipline

To be a warrior requires great discipline and obedience. One does not get to choose which orders one obeys. Military discipline requires instant obedience to every order. When we understand the warfare, the bride engages in, the need for obedience to the commands of the King becomes more important. She must know the heart of the King for a strategy to defeat the enemy. The King can perceive things she cannot, and she must hear from Him the correct move to take to stop the enemy in his nefarious schemes. People's lives depend on it.

The bride, as a warrior, underscores the importance prayer plays in the church's life. Prayer is not only making requests; prayer is listening. The bride stays in His presence until He shows a strategy, for the next step. It is pouring our hearts out to God and listening for Him to pour His heart out to us.

Somewhere in the worship/prayer exchange, He shows us how to triumph. First, we must learn for our own lives and then for the lives of others. She has shields enough for herself and to help train others. She is a city on a hill with battle advantage and the light of God within her.

Song 6:12. "Before I was aware, my soul set me over the chariots of my noble people."

Here we see chariots. Before the bride thinks, she found herself over the chariots of God's people. She has shields and chariots at her disposal so she wins in warfare. The bride has a battle strategy because she listens in the Secret Place. She leads the warrior's chariots because she knows the next moves of the King.

The Dancer Bride

Song 6:13 "Come back, come back, O Shulamite; Come back, come back, that we may gaze at you!" "Why should you gaze on the

Shulamite, as on the dance of Mahanaim?"

In the first part of the verse, the friends ask Shulamite to come back so they may watch her. They want to see her because, when they see her, they view the love, devotion, and glory of the Bridegroom Lamb. Christ shows forth in the believer's life, often based on how others come to desire Him. She is in warfare with the chariots, but now the friends ask for her, so they might grow in the things she has perfected.

The next part of the verse is the Bridegroom speaking. *"Why would you gaze on the bride as on the dance of Mahanaim?"*

The root word for Mahanaim means an encampment, an army of dancers, soldiers, etc. *[xxviii]* This refers to *Genesis 32:1-2 "Jacob also went on his way and the angels of God met him. When Jacob saw them he said, 'This is the camp of God!' So, he named that place Mahanaim."* Jacob was traveling to see Esau. Along the way, heavenly troops met Jacob's army, and they formed one army.

The bride is not alone in her battles. This is a fighting force of volunteers like her, willing to give all to know Him, and the angels of God fight with this army.

This verse shows her as a warrior who dances as a part of her warfare. She is the warrior dancer bride.

The Dancer

Once men would say
dance dancer dance.
She danced and served
and served and danced.
Joy was not in the dance,
not in the slave's dance.

Now she is set free
to dance for the King,
Set free from hard servitude.
Dance dancer dance.
Dance with joy,
the joy of the bride.

Not the obligation of the slave.
Dance dancer dance
There are victories to be won
for the King of love
Dance dancer dance.

Listen to the great choreographer
and dance the dance
He has written for you
No other dance will do.

As you dance before His love banner, the enemy is pushed
back.
He cannot withstand your beauty.
He cannot overcome your joy.
He cannot stop your love.
Your feet dance on the high places
of the earth.
You scale the places that
other feet cannot go.

Those are watching you
who cannot believe you
would be so loved.
They want to know
that what you know
is possible.

So, dance dancer dance
and win for your Love
the desire of His heart.
The company of dancers in the
earth that shine like the sun.

His people see him and love him. Their hearts sing, *"I belong
to my lover, and his desire is for me. "*They know the love of the
Bridegroom in its truth and glory. They are a force in the earth.

Every church age has known these people. Today, the Lord saved the best wine for last. This is truer today. Because the day we live in demands it.

This description is of the dancer he died to purchase. He invites us to be that dancer. Have you accepted the invitation? Will you accept it now?

Hear the rejoicing over the harlot's judgment and the readiness of the bride:

Rev.: 1 "After these things I heard something like a loud voice of a great multitude in heaven, saying, 'Hallelujah! Salvation and glory and power belong to our God;

Rev. 19:2 'BECAUSE HIS JUDGMENTS ARE TRUE AND RIGHTEOUS; for He has judged the great harlot who was corrupting the earth with her immorality, and HE HAS AVENGED THE BLOOD OF HIS BOND-SERVANTS ON HER.' Rev. 19:3 'And a second time they said, "Hallelujah! HER SMOKE RISES UP FOREVER AND EVER.'

Rev. 19:4 "And the twenty-four elders and the four living creatures fell down and worshiped God who sits on the throne saying, 'Amen. Hallelujah!'

Rev. 19:5 "And a voice came from the throne, saying, 'Give praise to our God, all you His bondservants, you who fear Him, the small and the great.6 Then I heard something like the voice of a great multitude and like the sound of many waters and like the sound of mighty peals of thunder, saying, 'Hallelujah! For the Lord our God, the Almighty, reigns. 7 'Let us rejoice and be glad and give the glory to Him, for the marriage of the Lamb has come and His bride has made herself ready. 8 It was given to her to clothe herself in fine linen, bright and clean; for the fine linen is the righteous acts of the saints.'

Rev. 19:9 "Then he said to me, Write, 'Blessed are those who are invited to the marriage supper of the Lamb.'" "And he said to me, "'These are true words of God."'

The bride makes herself ready. She is obedient, and as a result, she has received her garments from the King. She learns to dance the army dance. Because of her many joined the bride company.

Her prayers bring judgment on the harlot. She is in the company of the dancers of Mahanaim.

The two armies, the army of God and the bride company, are as one. No longer does she wonder how to draw near to her Lover because she walks near to Him constantly. Her every movement is under His direction. They dance, He leads, and she follows. See her dance in the earth with Him at the lead.

For Reflection

1. Are you ready to know the strategy of God to overcome the plan of the enemy in your life? How about the lives of others, in your city, in our nation?

2. Will you commit to fight and engage in warfare for the things that matter to God?

3. Will you allow your heart to become one with His so that when He takes a step, you follow? Will you dance in the earth with Him at the lead?

Prayer

Lord, I want to be the warrior dancer bride. Teach me the steps of obedience so I may dance your dance. Teach me how to press in not only for battle strategy but so I hear your voice in the Secret Place of Your presence. I want to follow Your every step and dance victories for You my King of Love.

CHAPTER 19
The Ready Bride

Psa. 45 states this about our King in verse *9, "At Your right hand stands the queen in gold from Ophir."* This bride is his people, clothed with the garments he provides. Solomon used the gold of Ophir [xxix] in armor, his throne, his house, and the temple. Ophir was "the" source of gold in Solomon's day. The King provides her clothing. Only royalty wore gold of Ophir. She stands at his right hand signifying she is a sheep and not a goat. Scripture tells us His sheep know His voice and they will not follow another. Those who know His voice spend much time with Him. He has clothed her in gold, signifying her purity and value to Him because of her whole-hearted devotion.

Forget Your Father's House

Then it speaks to us. *Psa. 45:10 "Listen, O daughter, give attention and incline your ear: Forget your people and your father's house;"*

To be ready, we, like this bride, must forget the futile way of life handed down to us from our forefathers. Since our futile way of life is our modus operandi, this directive is difficult. How can we find the strength and enlightenment we need to continue to leave behind these ways? She must forget the messages from her past that formed her incorrectly. Some messages have made her ugly on the inside and forgetting is imperative. Forgetting takes away the message's influence, so she is beautiful in those broken places.

1Pet. 1:18-19 18 "knowing that you were not redeemed with perishable things like silver or gold from your futile way of life inherited from your forefathers, 19 but with precious blood, as of a lamb unblemished and spotless, the blood of Christ."

Her redemption is total for the spotless Lamb redeems her. He gives her His fulness so she can choose new actions.

11 "Then the King will desire your beauty."

We need to know two things. First, we enthrall Him as we yield to Him and receive from Him the eye-salve, white garments and gold he provides. (Rev. 3) His smitten heart will sustain us if we seek him. He wants us to be much in His presence, for His heart desires us. The second thing is we honor Him in this seeking, and through this, we declare His Lordship over all we are — We bow to Him. Through submission, we will find enlightenment about our "stuff." Humility enables us to hear His voice, and His word bring freedom. Even so, maturity arrives when we forget our father's house.

"Because He is your Lord, bow down to Him." What His love must know is that she is so precious to Him He died for her. He is not only King but Lord and Judge. Because of His Lordship, she should bow down to Him. This means she puts His will first because she reverences His sacrifice and total obedience is the way she shows her love.

12 "The daughter of Tyre will come with a gift; The rich among the people will seek your favor." As a result of this total trust and submission, He gives the bride a place of influence with others. Now that desire for recognition and accolades are dead, He honors her. She has made Him Lord. He is her everything. His will is her way of living. He transforms her inner life, and the result follows in verse 13

13 "The King's daughter is all glorious within; She has no more residues left over from her father's house because he has set her free. Within He heals her, and she is glorious. Her glory shines for His glory shines through her life as she has become like Him for, she has seen Him in the Secret Place of His presence.

Her clothing is interwoven with gold. 14 She will be led to the King in embroidered work; The gold of Ophir is woven through her garments and her life. He has done this work in her. Her part was to yield to Him. She accepted the garments He had for her and His indwelling Spirit to bring healing, wholeness, and purifies the gold within her.

The virgins, her companions who follow her, will be brought to You. "On the wedding day in a Jewish marriage, the virgin companions waited with the bride until the Bridegroom came and led them to his house for the marriage feast. This feast is full of joy because the Bridegroom King has secured the love of His heart and creation and rejoices with Him.

Hear their song:

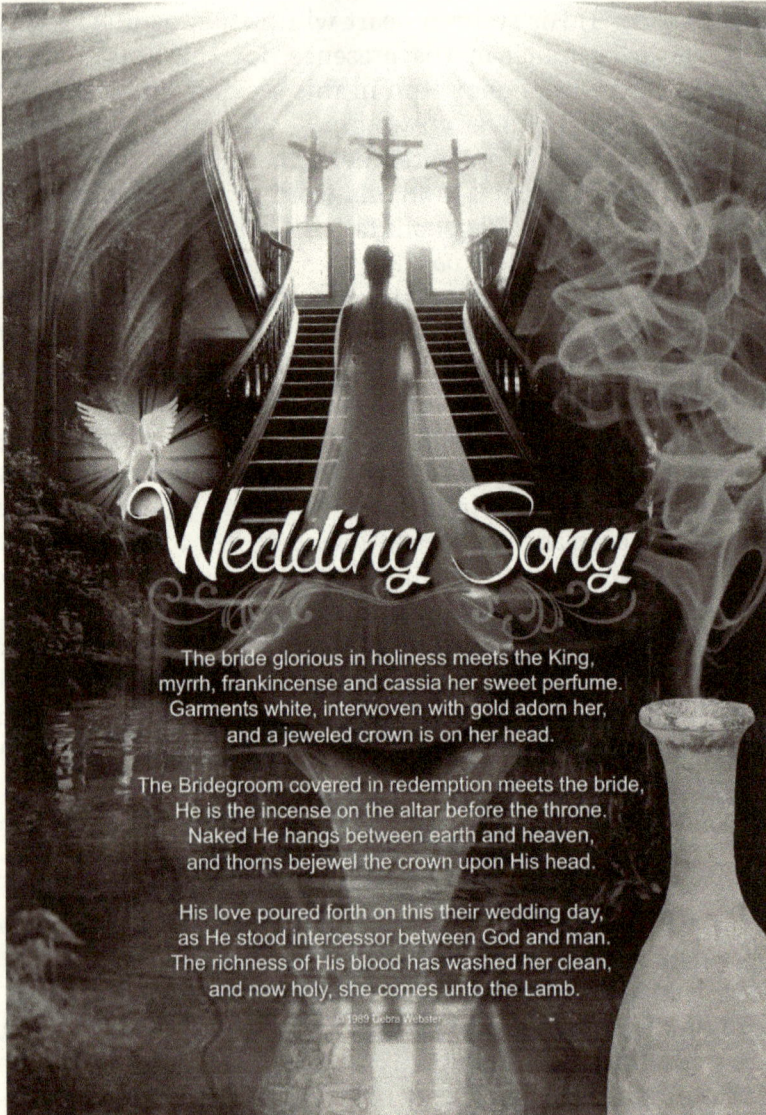

Wedding Song

The bride glorious in holiness meets the King,
myrrh, frankincense and cassia her sweet perfume.
Garments white, interwoven with gold adorn her,
and a jeweled crown is on her head.

The Bridegroom covered in redemption meets the bride,
He is the incense on the altar before the throne.
Naked He hangs between earth and heaven,
and thorns bejewel the crown upon His head.

His love poured forth on this their wedding day,
as He stood intercessor between God and man.
The richness of His blood has washed her clean,
and now holy, she comes unto the Lamb.

© 1989 Debra Webster

Receive this Secret Place truth. Remove the veils that separate you from Him. You are his.

2 Cor. 3:18 "But we all, with unveiled face, beholding as in a mirror the glory of the Lord, are being transformed into the same image from glory to glory, just as from the Lord, the Spirit."

Rev 19:7 "Let us rejoice and be glad and give the glory to Him, for the marriage of the Lamb has come and His bride has made herself ready."

For Reflection:

1. By searching the scriptures in this book and other scriptures that relate to the content, what can you do to realize change? Let the Lord show you the answers He desires in your life.

2. What areas of your attitude and beliefs are in error? What other gods do you serve? Do you fear rejection, poverty, exposure of your defectiveness, uncovering of your shame or sin? Do you give yourself to your electronics rather than the Lord? Write the other gods. What scriptures can you memorize (keep) to change your incorrect beliefs?

3. Do you believe you must perform to receive love? What does God say about His love for you? How can these truths help you? Record the things He is speaking to you. Then rehearse His truth until the enemy can no longer lie to you and say you must perform for love. Ref. Song 4:7, E Cor. 3:18, Ps.17:15, Phil. 3:7-8.

4 Ask the Lord to show you the place in His heart to which He calls you. Write what He says and make this the trajectory of your heart.

Prayer

Dear Bridegroom Lamb, I did not know my heart could still be so askew. I thought it was yours, but I see that is only partly true. Draw me and bring me into your presence, even if I resist. Show me the many gods I serve that keep me from seeing you. Help me focus on you.

Forgive me, my King, for my inability or unwillingness to see. I am blind but thought I see; wretched and thought it was normal. I am impoverished and thought I was rich. I am deceived and believed I was following truth. Today I ask to buy from you, gold refined in your fire and white clothing to cover my nakedness, and eye salve, so I see. Whatever the price of this I give you permission to receive that price from my life.

CHAPTER 20

THE GLORIOUS BRIDE

What follows describes the Lord's glorious bride.

Rev. 21:9 "Then one of the seven angels who had the seven-bowls full of the seven last plagues came and spoke with me, saying, 'Come here, I will show you the bride, the wife of the Lamb.' 10 And he carried me away in the Spirit to a great and high mountain, and showed me the holy city, Jerusalem, coming down out of heaven from God, 11 having the glory of God. Her brilliance was like a very costly stone, as a stone of crystal-clear jasper. 12 It had a great and high wall, with twelve gates, and at the gates twelve angels; and names were written on them, which are the names of the twelve tribes of the sons of Israel. 13 There were three gates on the east and three gates on the north and three gates on the south and three gates on the west. 14 And the wall of the city had twelve foundation stones, and on them were the twelve names of the twelve apostles of the Lamb."

It is significant that one angel who came to judge the harlot Babylon introduces the bride. Each of us that is part of the bride performs assigned tasks in obedience to the King much like the angel that took part in the harlot's judgment. Even when we find the task negative or difficult, we must fulfill it.

Since the angels in heaven rejoice over one repentant sinner, we can only imagine how the angels must have watched for the end of the harlot that led people astray. They know the desire of the Bridegroom's heart; that the bride comes forth in the glory she has received from Him. The angels know he is worthy, and they have waited for this culmination.

The Wife And The City

Not only does He introduce her as His bride, but scripture also calls her the wife of the Lamb. She is His eternal spouse and will live in intimate heart to heart relationship with Him eternally.

Then the angel presents her as a city shining with the glory of God. She has twelve gates, three on each side with the names of the twelve tribes of Israel and twelve foundations with the names of the Apostles of the Lamb.

This city comprises true believers from all times. The Apostles laid the foundation; we build the city upon the foundation. Until the Lamb came and died, no one understood the Old Testament prophecies well. It was in the Lamb's sacrifice that we could consider the past and His great love.

Indeed, this city could not be complete without the twelve tribes of Israel, those who believed in Old Testament times and the 12 Apostles of the Lamb. Belief in every age includes obedience and intimacy.

Rev. 21:15 "The one who spoke with me had a gold measuring rod to measure the city, and its gates and its wall. 16 The city is laid out as a square, and its length is as great as the width; and he measured the city with the rod, fifteen hundred miles; its length and width and height are equal. 17 And he measured its wall, seventy-two yards, according to human measurements, which are also angelic measurements. 18 The material of the wall was jasper; and the city was pure gold, like clear glass. 19 The foundation stones of the city wall were adorned with every kind of precious stone. The first foundation stone was jasper; the second, sapphire; the third, chalcedony; the fourth, emerald; 20 the fifth, sardonyx; the sixth, sardius; the seventh, chrysolite; the eighth, beryl; the ninth, topaz; the tenth, chrysoprase; the eleventh, jacinth; the twelfth, amethyst. 21 And the twelve gates were twelve pearls; each one of the gates was a single pearl. And the street of the city was pure gold, like transparent glass."

The angel measured the city. It was 1500 miles high, wide and long. It is a four square vast and glorious city. This is the shape of the Temple's Holy of Holies. It was a perfect cube. This heavenly city is the real. The Holy of Holies in the Temple was a type. Thus, this city was in God's heart from time's beginning. Everything that occurred in history was to culminate in the bringing forth of this eternal city, the eternal dwelling of the bride of the Lamb.

Those who hunger for the intimacy He calls us to as His bride know the Temple and the Holy of Holies help them understand how to enter God's presence. Their heart's cry goes something like this:

The Secret Place
Lamp-stand, showbread, only types of Him
Into whose presence, I must now come.

Not trusting the ritual of the stand and bread.
But looking unto Him in that Secret Place.

Putting aside all types and shadows,
facsimiles and caricatures of Him.

What my mind thinks will not suffice.
My eye must behold Him in the Secret Place.

Then I will know who He really is.
Not just what men would say
or types and shadows show.

Then will I learn to be content
in Him
only in Him.

The walls are pure gold, the foundations are 12 different precious stones and the twelve gates are 12 pearls. This contrasts with cities of ancient days with dirt streets, stonewalls and opens sewers. The pearl gates speak of purity. The streets of this city are pure gold, like transparent glass. This gold is beyond the pure gold of our day. Though we could see our reflection in pure gold, we cannot see through it as if transparent. Because this city's purity is beyond comprehension, just as the holiness of God is unfathomable.

The Lamb is the Lamp

Rev. 21:22 "I saw no temple in it, for the Lord God the Almighty and the Lamb are its temple.23 And the city has no need of the sun or of the moon to shine on it, for the glory of God has illumined it, and its lamp is the Lamb.24 The nations will walk by its light, and the kings of the earth will bring their glory into it.25 in the daytime (for there will be no night there) its gates will never be closed; 26 and they will bring the glory and the honor of the nations into it; 27 and nothing unclean, and no one who practices abomination and lying, shall ever come into it, but only those whose names are written in the Lamb's book of life."

This city needs no sun or moon or light of any kind. Like the Holy of Holies, the glory of God gives it light, and the Lamb is its lamp. The bride is preparing even now as she spends time with God in the Secret Place, the Holy of Holies of His presence. In fact, she is giving her time and her life, allowing Him to change her until His glory transforms her. Then she ministers to others out of that place, and they also desire Him. They want Him because they view His glory in her. Nothing unclean will enter this city, rather only those whose names are written in the Lamb's book will inhabit it.

The Water of Life

Rev. 22:1 "Then he showed me a river of the water of life, clear as crystal, coming from the throne of God and of the Lamb, 2 in the middle of its street On either side of the river was the tree of life, bearing twelve kinds of fruit, yielding its fruit every month and the leaves of the tree were for the healing of the nations.3 There will no longer be any curse; and the throne of God and of the Lamb will be in it, and His bond-servants will serve Him; 4 they will see His face, and His name will be on their foreheads.5 And there will no longer be any night; and they will not have need of the light of a lamp nor the light of the sun, because the Lord God will illumine them; and they will reign forever and ever."

Next, we notice a river of the water of life and the tree of life yielding year-round fruit. No more will the tree of knowledge defile humanity. No more will we struggle with the sin nature. Rather, God broke the curse for eternity. God's throne is present, and He will rule forever with His Beloved Bride.

Bride City Of God

The King reigns and

His glory shines from

the city of His heart.

The focal point of heaven

is this city.

His throne dwells there.

His light illuminates every corner.

The emerald rainbow lights her.

The sea of glass illumines her.

Glory shines from her,

like refined gold,

like purified transparent gold.

The King is her only light.

She carries His heart.

History ends, and eternity begins. Are you willing to get ready? "The Spirit and the bride sav come." The Bridearoom

ABOUT THE AUTHOR

"Forty years in the wilderness is God's way. If we argue with Him about it, He wins. I argued even before I knew it would be so long. He won the argument, and I am so glad He did. He is God. I had to learn that and still am learning. How good He knows us, expects it and is not moved by our complaints. He just is and therefore I am."

Debra hears the Lord in the Secret Place concerning His bride He gave her a message for the church in this day. There is no message more important for the church today, because this is a message for the bride of His heart. It is the Bridegroom seeing His bride. He sought her before He made her in Eden and as she keeps her focus on Him resisting the enemies plan, she will be forever His.

Website: https://bridesheart.com

Author page: http://amazon.com/author/debrawebster

Bibliography

[i] Unger's Bible Dictionary, The New Unger's Bible Dictionary (Unger's Dictionary), by Merrill F. Unger, R. K. Harrison, editor, Used by permission of Moody Bible Institute of Chicago, All rights reserved.

[ii] Smiths's Bible Dictionary, 1889, Public Domain

[iii] Strong's Exhaustive Concordance of the Bible, Public Domain

[iv] Ibid.

[v] Ibid.

[vi] NIV Dictionary New American Standard Bible Update, Copyright ©1960, 1962, 1963,1968, 1971, 1972, 1973, 1975, 1977, 1995 by The Lockman Foundation, All rights reserved, New American Standard Bible, 1995 edition, with Strong's numbers., Version 3.7

[vii] Ibid.

[viii] Ibid.

[ix] Ibid. Unger's

[x] Ibid.

[xi] IVP Bible Background Commentary: New Testament (IVP-NT Commentary), © 1993 by Craig S. Keener,
Electronic text hypertexted and prepared by OakTree Software, Inc., Version 2

[xii] Webster's New Collegiate Dictionary, Public Domain

[xiii] Ibid. Strong's

[xiv]IVP Bible Background Commentary: New Testament
© 2000 by John H. Walton, Victor H. Matthews and Mark W. Chavalas

[xv] Ibid. Strong'

[xvi] Ibid. IVP NT Background Commentary

[xvii] Eerdmans Dictionary of the Bible, David Noel Freedman, Editor-in-Chief, © 2000 Wm. B. Eerdmans Publishing Co.
All rights reserved, Electronic text hypertexted and prepared by OakTree Software, Inc., Version 3.6

[xviii] The Veiled Ploy, John Paul Jackson

[xix] Ibid. Strong's

[xx] Ibid. Strong's

[xxi]

[xxii]The Ryrie Study Bible — Expanded Edition, by Charles Caldwell Ryrie., © 1986 & 1995 by The Moody Bible Institute of Chicago.

[xxiii]Ibid. Unger's

[xxiv] Ibid Strong's

[xxv] by John MacArthur, Copyright ©1985-2009 by The Moody Bible Institute of Chicago. All rights reserved.

[xxvi] Ibid. Ungers

[xxvii] Ibid. Strong's

[xxviii]Ibid. Strong's

[xxix] Ibid, Unger's

www.ingramcontent.com/pod-product-compliance
Lightning Source LLC
LaVergne TN
LVHW011206080426
835508LV00007B/621